FROM **INCESTUOUS CHRISTIANITY** TO MAKING DISCIPLES

UNLEASH THE **POWER** OF **THE GOSPEL** BY **EVANGELIZING AT LEAST ONE SUNDAY A MONTH**

UDO F. NWACHUKWU

Published by Udo F. Nwachukwu

Library of Congress Control Number: 2019902782

ISBN-13: 978-1-7337091-0-1 (paperback)
ISBN-13: 978-1-7337091-1-8 (Ebook)
ISBN-13: 978-1-7337091-2-5 (Kindle)

Unless otherwise noted, all Bible citations are from the New King James Version®. Copyright © 1982 by Thomas Nelson. Used by permission. All rights reserved.

Cover and interior design by Rob Williams, InsideOutCreativeArts.com

For additional information please visit www.udoministries.com
or e-mail the author at ambassador2dworld@gmail.com.

DEDICATION

This book is dedicated to my Lord and Savior, Jesus Christ, who died for me and gave His life for me. No one else has ever volunteered to die for me, so all honor and glory goes to Jesus, the lover of my soul, and to almighty God, my Father, and to my helper, God the Holy Spirit. Thank you, Lord, for choosing and electing me to be Your child even before the foundation of the world. It humbles me to think that You thought about me before I came to be. I long for You, and at the appointed day, I shall see You face to face, never to be separated from You for eternity.

I also dedicate this book to all my natural and spiritual fathers and mothers, plus my natural and spiritual brothers and sisters who have nurtured me into faith in Christ. You've also let me know that I belong to Him. Thank you all.

Table of Contents

Preface

This book would not have been written except for Pastor Phil's preaching and stirring of my heart. Back in 2013, he preached a series on being radical for Christ based on the book *Radical* by David Platt. Until recently, Phil Powers was the lead pastor of Forcey Bible Church in Silver Spring, Maryland, which is where I attend.

I was captivated by the truth of the messages that were reflections of the truths found in Scripture as lived out by the early church and the disciples in the book of Acts. The lingering question for me then and now is: *What is radical and how can we be radical for Christ in the twenty-first century?* My thought was that if we are going to be radical, then let's be radical and challenge our tradition and go outside the box. Let's be radical in the way we do and are church. Let's set aside at least one Sunday a month to go to our neighbors and pray with them and tell them about Jesus and His good news of the gospel. I sent Phil a note expressing my appreciation for his insights and to also communicate my thought and idea.

Three years passed. I suffered a stroke and was in recovery. In God's divine sovereignty and circumstances, I was homebound with enough time to think, reflect and pray.

I arranged to meet with Phil to remind him of the crazy, radical idea I wrote him about three years before. He heard me out and, like the good former professor he is, started asking me some basic questions, such as consequences and implications of my at-least-one-Sunday-a-month-going-out-to-evangelize idea. With those questions and the Holy Spirit stirring me, I responded that I needed to write down what has been revealed to me so that I could answer his questions. That conversation was the genesis of this book.

This book examines where we are as the church in our state of what I call "incestuous Christianity." It proposes setting aside at least one Sunday a month to make the gospel a priority for the church and, in turn, inspire individuals to greater personal evangelism. I give examples on how it has been done in the past and how it can be done in the present through door-to-door evangelism.

In 2017, we celebrated 500 years of a Reformation that was initiated by Martin Luther through his simple but bold action of challenging the church tradition of his time. Through that movement, the Bible was printed in the vernacular and made available for the masses to read and live by. I believe we are not done challenging the church traditions. It is now time for the Bible's core message, the gospel (Christ crucified for our sins, rising and coming again), to be lived out and preached by all God's people to this dying world. "Go and make disciples" is for all believers and Christ's followers to obey without exception.

Stoyan Zaimov, reporting in *The Christian Post* on a new study released in December 2017, wrote, "The percentage of born-again Christians in America continues declining, a major religious survey has found." This decline has been attributed to only 39 percent of born-again Christians affirming and owning up to the responsibility of sharing the gospel. To this, pollster George Barna said, "Christianity in America is going through a time of substantial challenge. The Church at-large is not likely to grow in the future unless some fundamental changes in practice are made." This book is offering one of those fundamental changes. The true Church of Christ is still those who are "born again" (John 3:3); that is, reborn again from above by the Holy Spirit regardless of denomination.

We never know how long we have to do something for God. On September 16, 2017, at the relatively young age of 34, our brother in Christ Nabeel Qureshi went home to be with Jesus. I thank God for Nabeel's short life and love for Jesus. His accomplishments as a Christian apologist have inspired and quickened my steps to finish this book without further delay and to live the life I now have to the fullest for Christ. He wrote *Seeking Allah, Finding Jesus: A Devout Muslim's Journey to Christ.*

God transformed Nabeel from the kingdom of darkness of an Islamic background to His marvelous light in Christ Jesus, just as He did for each of us.

Ravi Zacharias, the Christian apologist and president of the Ravi Zacharias International Ministries, worked with Nabeel and said of him, "It is amazing that a life so brief had an impact so big." To God be the glory for Nabeel's testimony and for all who have come to faith in Christ and still will in reading one of his books.

So, let's go, church, in the power of the Holy Spirit and through Christ who gives us strength to win the lost for Christ. We do not have much time and we don't know when it will be our time to depart. Oh yes, the lost, the unbeliever in Christ, will be in hell according to Scripture.

Introduction

This book is an expression of God's desire for us, His church and children, to do what He has always asked us to do. To believe in Christ is to know Him and make Him known. The early church did well in this regard, but we have slacked off. This book is a manifesto for a movement to revive the church once again and help us do what we are supposed to do. This simple manual aims to shake up the current church structure and ways of being and doing church. This is not for pastors who want to maintain the status quo, nor is it for people of God who view church as a resting place to only be comforted and catered to. This book is a manual for *intentionally* working and laboring in the Father's harvest of souls and for being Holy Spirit-driven in doing so.

Let's get going, church, and use our ample resources to go out and tell people the gospel. Let's give up our pews and pulpits at least one Sunday a month and go to the byways and highways (and door to door) where the people are to tell them the good news of Christ the Savior and Redeemer. Enough "soaking;" it is time to squeeze the sponge! As with baby birds in a cozy nest, it is time for the mother bird to push them out so they can fly, preach, live out the gospel and experience real joy in doing so. Dear pastors, priests, general overseers, bishops, popes, board members and all leaders of the body of Christ: As it says in Exodus 8:1, "Let my people go that they may truly worship and serve Me."

Yes, the church, its pastors and leaders are working hard and doing many good things. We thank God for all the hard work. But have we left our first love for Jesus Christ and His command to seek and save the lost? Why do we get caught up with ingatherings in our buildings and cathedrals? Let us go back to the first things we did in the beginning. I love and have benefited from the various wonderful teachings and equipping by gifted men and women of God. But the equipping is for the purpose of the work of ministry. What greater work is there than sharing the gospel of Christ?

God is now ready to use all of our past preparation to support His end-time harvest. Every hand must be on the job and not just a few.

"Go," is one of Jesus' last instructions in Matthew 28: "Go and make disciples." It has not changed. We owe a debt of gratitude to our Lord Jesus Christ who poured out Himself for us. This is our motivation and nothing more and no one else to impress. Let's love Him back through our obedience and by actually obeying the Greatest Commission.

Jesus would say to us just as He said to Peter, "Do you love Me? . . . Feed my sheep" (John 21:17), and to all His disciples, "Peace to you! As the Father has sent Me, I also send you . . . Receive the Holy Spirit. If you forgive the sins of any, they are forgiven them; if you retain the sins of any, they are retained" (John 20:21-23), and in Luke 6:46, "Why do you call me 'Lord, Lord,' and not do what I say? . . . You are my friends if you do what I command."

We all can pray and cry for revival until we are blue in our faces. The key to revival is obedience to the great commission of preaching and living the gospel. There is nothing else to revive us to than to obey and do that which Christ came for and died to do. Obedience brings the fire in us. Obedience of going out is better than the sacrifices in our polished edifices of church buildings. On obedience, A. W. Tozer had this to say:

It is my conviction that much, very much, prayer for and talk about revival these days is wasted energy. Ignoring the confusion of figures, I might say that it is hunger that appears to have no object; it is dreamy wishing that is too weak to produce moral action. It is fanaticism on a high level for, according to John Wesley, "a fanatic is one who seeks desired ends while ignoring the constituted means to reach those ends."

The correction of this error is extremely difficult for it entails more than a mere adjustment of our doctrinal beliefs; it strikes at the whole Adam-life and requires self-abnegation, humility and cross carrying. In short it requires obedience. And that we will do anything to escape.

It is almost unbelievable how far we will go to avoid obeying God. We call Jesus "Lord" and beg Him to rejuvenate our souls, but we are careful to do not the things He says. When faced with a sin, a confession or a moral alteration in our life, we find it much easier to pray half a night than to obey God.

I could not have said it any better. I don't want to end my life being a religious fanatic who sees what needs to be done, how it should be done, but still refuses to follow through to the end goal of telling people the gospel of Christ. I do not wish the same for you as an individual or as a corporate church entity.

The Lord is full of blessings and loves to give to us. Blessing will initially attract us to God but we go beyond blessings. We will find God Himself. Then we can see Him for who He is and not just for the blessings. In fact, God is the blessing we seek and through us the nations and peoples are blessed.

When we meet with God, He reveals Himself to us. Then we understand His heart and what He longs for. God longs for His children to be gathered to Him. This is where mission and outreach begin. It begins in the heart of the Father God.

Our gospel outreach is not a mechanical going but worship and an expression of our love relationship with the Father, Son and Holy Spirit. After all, the Holy Spirit is the one who is leading us out, who speaks the Father's words, and who brings conviction, repentance and reconciliation to the Lord God.

Our goal, like the apostle Paul, is to be well pleasing to our Father in all that we do and say. There is nothing greater that touches our Father's heart than to help bring into His kingdom His children for whom His only begotten Son died. We are being offered a lifetime opportunity to work alongside of God to accomplish what He has already ordained.

The world we live in is disintegrating fast and we are seeing all kinds of evils being perpetuated by heartless people in shootings, killings, government corruption, and stealing by professional thieves using guns and pens to acquire wealth meant for the public good. Racial/tribal tensions and hatred are occurring regularly in almost every part of the globe. We are seeing drug use and overdoses becoming epidemics in the West. People no longer have a purpose for living. Families are breaking up at the highest rates, and immorality and alternative lifestyles of same-sex marriage are now the thing of the day and the law of some nations. We cannot stand on the sidelines and look for political saviors to legislate morality. We have abandoned our responsibility and are asking the politicians to do the work of the church. We must intentionally reach the people and change the world we live in through the power of the gospel. As Proverbs 14:34 says, "Righteousness exalts a nation, but sin is a reproach to any nation and people." Christ is our righteousness. He has already died for the sins of the world.

Let's go, church!

1

Why Bother Knocking?

I have heard many stories from modern times that inspire people to evangelism. By evangelism, I mean speaking or presenting the gospel to the one who has not come to faith and trust in Christ. Maybe we can relate to the stories of our time because we can see ourselves in them. Of course, there are no greater narratives than the accounts in the Bible, such as when the apostles in the book of Acts were moved by the Holy Spirit to preach and saw tremendous numbers of people being added to the church daily.

Really, why bother knocking? For one thing, the folks in hell are concerned. In Luke 16:19-31, the rich man in hell was burdened for his family and requested for someone to go and tell them, "lest they also come to this place of torment." The hell torment is forever, so how much more should we, who are alive and heading to heaven, care about these people? Do we really believe there is a hell and that people who have not trusted Christ's finished work on the cross for salvation will go there? There is no need to preach the gospel if there is no hell, or if we do not believe there is a hell.

Many of us have had someone who have died before we mustered the courage to tell him/her about the gospel. The chance is gone and we cannot do anything about missed opportunities except to repent. Now we can do something and tell someone else before it is too late.

Someone is waiting to receive an invitation and be introduced to Jesus Christ, the Savior. But some think door-to-door evangelism is out of date and not for our times. In his article published in *Desiring God* and titled "Evangelism on the Rocks," Jonathan Dodson, pastor of City Life Church in Austin, Texas, gives this grim description of present-day evangelism in America:

Evangelism is something many Christians are trying to recover from.

The word stirs up memories of a bygone era—some call it "Christendom"—where rehearsed presentations, awkward door-to-door witnessing, a steady flow of tracts, and conversions in revival-like settings were commonplace. As American culture becomes increasingly fragmented and secularized, these forms of evangelism create an impediment to the Gospel.

Wave after wave of rationalistic, rehearsed (and at times coerced and confrontational) evangelism inoculates, if not antagonizes, the broader society. The Gospel is slowly associated with forceful Christians who are information-driven, looking to get Jesus off their chest. As a result, evangelism is viewed as an attempt to recruit converts, not love our neighbors.

Dodson goes on to suggest necessary changes to make the gospel believable by learning a new language or metaphors for a generation that does not believe there is a God. He further said that we must package the gospel to a generation divided into "seekers of acceptance," "seekers of hope," "seekers of intimacy," and "seekers of tolerance." While I agree that we must make the gospel believable and tailored to this generation's perceived needs, we still need methods to engage the people. Where do we meet folks besides the people we know through friendship? On average, how many unbelievers of Christ do we know or are acquainted with? Not too many! We must still go to this generation that sees the Christian as an antagonist. We cannot callously say, "Leave them alone; it is their business."

The old methods that Dodson relegates to the "bygone era" of "Christendom" are still relevant and they still work. We still need to give out the tracts. Going door to door may be awkward but it still works because we do not recruit converts but instead introduce people to Jesus. Only Jesus can convert a soul. Our experience and those of others going door to door have proven that people still welcome a church that cares enough to knock at their doors to pray with them and tell them the good news of the gospel. In chapter 11 of this book, I show the results of door-to-door evangelism by a Kentucky church that tripled attendance in six months. It is still effective, especially in this generation when face time has been reduced greatly by social media. People are still happy to see other human beings instead of electronic pictures.

We must never be intimidated by the analysis of the experts who have not motivated the church to go to the people. We do not want to be robotic in our presentation, nor appear coerced and confrontational. However, we must also never forget that the gospel is offensive because of its truth, and we cannot water that down. We must in humility continue to go to the people with the gospel because many of us also used to be antagonistic to Christ and to followers of Christ.

I was delighted when my editor, Julia Duin, called my attention to a recent article in *The Washington Post* written by Julie Zauzmer and titled "Fishing for another 'like': At Easter, many Christians return to door-to-door methods." Zauzmer talked about many churches in the Washington region and across the country returning to this supposed old-fashioned method because of the results. Friends, going door to door still works!

Still looking for a reason to obey Jesus' command to make disciples?

Rico Tice, associate minister at All Souls Langham Place, London, wrote a book called *Honest Evangelism: How to talk about Jesus even when it's tough*. He makes the point that God has placed us in this time period, in this generation, in our localities and jobs, and even in our countries for the purposes of seeking and finding God. Then, through us, others will seek and find God. Rico calls it "God's sovereignty." He cites Acts 17:24-28, where Paul spoke to the thinkers of his day at the Areopagus in Athens. Paul said:

> God, who made the world and everything in it, since He is Lord of heaven and earth, does not dwell in temples made with hands. Nor is He worshiped with men's hands, as though He needed anything, since He gives to all life, breath, and all things. And He has made from one blood every nation of men to dwell on all the face of the earth, and has determined their pre-appointed times and the boundaries of their dwellings, so that they should seek

the Lord, in the hope that they might grope for Him and find Him, though He is not far from each one of us; for in Him we live and move and have our being, as also some of your own poets have said, "For we are also His offspring."

The implication of the above scripture is that there are no co-incidences in the lives of followers of Christ nor those who have yet to put their trust in Christ. People are in our lives by God's sovereign arrangement, and if they do not know Christ, then we are there to point them to Him. The same is true for every church location. The church is in a particular locale for God's divine purpose that must be accomplished in that neighborhood.

Our goal is to honor and worship our Father in all that we do, including preaching the gospel. We have been made for this sole purpose: to worship God. I was reminded of this as I read Mark Clifton's book *Reclaiming Glory: Revitalizing Dying Churches*. In this, Clifton cites John Piper in his book *Let the Nations Be Glad!* Piper wrote:

Missions is not the ultimate goal of the church. Worship is. Mission exists because worship doesn't. Worship is the ultimate, not missions, because God is ultimate, not man. When this age is over, and the countless millions of the redeemed fall on their faces before the throne of God, missions will be no more. It is a temporary necessity. But worship abides forever. Worship, therefore, is the fuel and goal of missions. It's the goal of missions because in missions we simply aim to bring the nations into the white-hot enjoyment of God's glory. The goal of missions is the gladness of the peoples in the greatness of God.

Well said, Mr. Piper. May we forever keep this picture in our minds and in front of us. We, all humans, were created in God's image to worship Him. God is already glorious and we can't add to that, but rather we come to behold Him and enjoy His glory forever. We don't want anyone to miss forever, the glory of God.

It is good to be inspired by modern-day stories or by the Scriptures. We can equally read the expert opinions and dismiss all the known, old-fashioned means of evangelism and preaching of the gospel. The question is, how are we doing as individuals and as the corporate body of Christ instead? What is our present state of obedience to the Great Commission?

2

Incestuous Christianity

Yes, you heard that right. I wish the title of this chapter could have had a more politically correct, less shocking word than "incestuous." It was a word that was dropped in my spirit as I lay awake meditating on the state of the church. Incestuous Christianity is inbred Christianity where we are satisfied in taking care of ourselves but are distasteful to God. The Lord is close to throwing up! We think we are making progress, but we are going nowhere. We think we are growing, but we are stunted because of the inbred DNA that keeps getting weaker every day and becomes more prone to disease.

I know the word "incest" makes people uncomfortable. Like in many families where incest has been perpetrated, it is usually hush hush. No one wants to talk about it. It is a dark family secret hidden from everyone and from the next generation. Evil thrives in darkness; that is why everyone and every deed must come under the light of Christ so that we can receive forgiveness, healing and restoration. The church, being a family, must deal with any sin in the family of believers. Let judgment begin in the house of God.

Incest is forbidden by the Lord in Leviticus 18. Those who cause it (mostly men) are sick and self-absorbed. Such people only think of themselves and focus on self-gratification. The same can apply to a people or a church and that is where we are today. Let's examine some cases of incest from the Bible.

Lot and His Daughters
While the world (Sodom and Gomorrah) engaged in homosexuality and received God's judgment, the people of God turned and committed incest. Lot abhorred the deeds of the people of Sodom and Gomorrah. God, by His sovereign grace, brought Lot's family out from the city before destroying it. Rather than trusting God, they were filled with selfish interest and self-preservation. The daughters of Lot got their father drunk and had sex with him. The resulting children were not blessed and could not be counted among God's people of Israel (see Deuteronomy 23:3).

Part of the problem was Lot's wife, who looked back instead of going forward and turned into a pillar of salt (see Genesis 19:26). Had she been present with her family, there would have been no incest! Some churches have turned into pillars of salt and are no longer useful for God's purposes. These churches have become monuments for sightseeing and Sunday outings. These churches are all over the world, especially in the West. Anything goes in the name of tolerance and accommodation. They never want to offend anyone, and they want to be politically correct.

These "Lot's wife" churches ordain practicing homosexuals as ministers and thus have lost the spiritual authority to speak against such sins. The homosexual as well as the adulterer are, of course, welcomed first to Christ, just like any of us, but they must be encouraged to encounter Christ's cleansing and transformation. We cannot continue in sin that grace may abound. Apostle Paul said "God forbid" a lot. These churches are marrying same-sex couples and they don't see anything wrong in it.

Back to Lot: By the grace of God, the angels grasped the hands of his family members and dragged them out of Sodom and Gomorrah. But they engaged in incest and produced the Moabites and the Ammonites, who never ceased fighting the Israelites, as we discover in Joshua 24. Also, the gods of the Moabites and Ammonites were constant distractions to the people of Israel who sought them (see Judges 10:6).

These days, many in the church are worshiping the "other gods" of the Moabites and the Ammonites. Joshua warned the Israelites of this in Joshua 24:14-15.

Notice that Lot and his daughters were to dwell where the people were as God granted him his request. Genesis 19:21-22,30 says, "'Very well, I will grant this request too; I will not overthrow the town you speak of. But flee there quickly, because I cannot do anything until you reach it.' (That is why the town was called Zoar) . . . Lot and his two daughters left Zoar and settled in the mountains, for he was afraid to stay in Zoar." Instead, they left the place of safety and the protection of God and isolated themselves in the mountains in a cave. They were "afraid" and, in addition, Lot thought the place was too small, for *Zoar* means "small."

The church today is afraid of going to where the people are; in their neighborhoods and homes. We have rather chosen to dwell in our self-made caves of church buildings. The fear and lack of desire to step out of the church building is the recipe for incest and stunted growth that we see presently. It will never glorify God. Lot was also looking for a bigger place, the same as we are doing today. Build it big to seat 5,000 to 10,000, as if God is impressed with the size of our buildings and as if the size determines the presence of God.

I believe Lot's daughters would have been properly married if they had dwelled in Zoar, and they would have produced righteous offspring. Fear is crippling the church of today from going to the people who need the church—that is, the people of Zoar, who do not know God. We quickly forget we all used to live in Zoar (sin city), but for the grace of God, He saved us and made us His own.

Amnon and Tamar

Another example of incest is the case of King David's son Amnon, who raped his half-sister Tamar. He burned with lust and passion for her and could only think of himself. The result was discord and murder of Amnon by Tamar's brother Absalom. Nothing good comes out of forbidden incestuous relationship.

The whole story is relayed in 2 Samuel 13. What a story and plot! Hollywood could not do any better than this mini movie where eventually Absalom had Amnon assassinated at a party.

Many churches are passionate about church growth but not passionate about evangelism and obeying the great commission of "go and make disciples." Like Amnon, who consulted "Jonadab," who "was a very crafty man" (2 Samuel 13:3), churches will consult with all the church growth experts who have not helped most churches in real growth. Some churches will go out of their way to entice and attract believers from other churches with such gimmicks as changing the lighting or ramping up the music, and providing childcare and programs for every age group.

The churches refuse to ask the Father, the King, for harvesters/workers to go to unbelievers outside the camp to gather them and bring them into the kingdom. Tamar is still crying for the church today to "'Please speak to the king; he will not keep me from being married to you.' But he refused to listen to her, and since he was stronger than she, he raped her." Will we heed her plea?

Amnon could have married any girl in Israel outside of his family just for the asking. Think of the wonderful children who could have come from Amnon, but who never came to be. What about Tamar? She never married and never recovered from the devastation. How many are "desolate" in our churches of today from things they have endured via the hands of money-hungry ministers and church people who used and abused them? We cannot remain desolate forever. Jesus is here to heal and restore wholeness to His people.

This incestuous sin of Amnon had almost an unending chain reaction. Absalom murdered him and fled to another part of the country and started his own church. Absalom started to entice the people of the kingdom in competition with his father, King David. Eventually, he was killed by Joab, his father's top military commander.

Why do you think we have so many denominations and so many mushroom churches these days? You need to go to the developing countries such as Nigeria, about which I can speak as an eyewitness. In most major cites of southeastern and western Nigeria, you may have up to five churches within a short block. Most of these churches were started by the disgruntled and wounded from other churches. There is intense competition for the existing believers from other churches with promise/enticement of the prosperity gospel. It is same in the western world to some degree.

Reuben and His Father's Wife

There are actually consequences of incest that result to a church or person never reaching their potential. Of course, there is always repentance and forgiveness from our Father, but we cannot undo some consequences of past sin. There is always a new beginning in Christ and that is what we seek for us as individuals and as a corporate church body. If we truly own up and repent of our sins, God will use our messes as a message to the world to show them that Jesus' cleansing power of sanctification is effective and working by His grace even in the church of today.

Reuben could never reach his potential because he slept with his father's concubine, Bilhah (see Genesis 35:21-22; 49:3-4). The sons born by Bilhah were Jacob's and were half-brothers to Reuben; thus, Bilhah—though a concubine—was equivalent to a wife. At his death bed, Jacob declared to Reuben that he was "unstable as water, you shall not excel."

Likewise, Paul rebuked the church in Corinth that tolerated incest. A man slept with his father's wife and the church was living in so much denial that they could not see anything wrong (see 1 Corinthians 5:1). All these examples point to a common thread: self-gratification and self-absorption. There were no desires to do God's will in His designed way.

We are jumping from one congregation to another, playing church like musical chairs. We fool ourselves with empty growth. We spend lots of time and resources debating the type of music/worship (traditional or contemporary). We even grumble and leave one congregation for the other because of the color of carpet chosen by the building committee. We move to a new congregation because they have just finished a brand-new building that has facilities for all age groups. Who does not like new buildings? But when did that become the criteria for belonging to a particular congregation?

We come together to inoculate ourselves with the same vaccine that makes us feel good but does not heal us. We have become so good in sermonizing and making people feel good with what they want to hear. At the same time, the people lack the real joy of the Lord. We feed them the prosperity and political gospels and all the self-help doctrines on financial success and getting out of debt—theories on marriage, happiness forever, various "breakthrough" principles, etc. When they like what we are saying, they stay. Once they disagree, they move on to the next congregation. The new home congregation celebrates pseudo-church growth. We do this Sunday after Sunday, year after year.

Now, it is okay to come to church to be healed and blessed and to seek blessing. Most of us come for that reason. But it cannot be the only thing we do and the primary thing we do. Blessings are byproducts of seeking first His kingdom and preaching the gospel. God is not anti-prosperity. He wants us to prosper, but in His own way: by seeking Him first and making building His kingdom our priority (see Matthew 6:33). Building His kingdom is not the same thing as building a church building; it's building people for His glory.

Lord, we repent. Help us and revive us and heal us. Father, unleash the power of the gospel in us and among us in our communities, states, countries, and the entire world.

At a Personal Level

At this point, I would say that the Spirit of Christ does not condemn but sets the captives free. If the material in this section of the book has brought back memories at a personal level and you had been involved in any form of incest and have not dealt with it in reconciliation with our Father God, then this is a good time to come clean and receive forgiveness and refreshing from our Christ who died for us. This may begin a journey of healing and reconciliation for you as perpetrator and also for the one who was violated. As a perpetrator, you may have to seek forgiveness from the one wronged, especially if they are still living.

On the other hand, if you have been violated in your family as a result of incest and you are still carrying the heavy weight of guilt, shame and blame, now is also a good time to be freed by the cleansing blood of Jesus. Maybe you have never told anyone. Go ahead now and talk with Jesus, who alone understands. Seek Christian counseling and get any necessary help. This book was not written in any way to shame anyone but to set us free as a people of God that we may be used to set others free by what we have experienced ourselves, both corporately and individually.

3

Out-of-focus and
Inward-focused Church

We have used the church resources for everything but for going and making disciples of Christ. If the gospel is the core business of the church, where does it show? We expect people to show up at our church doors on their own volition so we can preach to them. Even when one or two trickle in, good luck if they ever hear the gospel preached in clear terms. Yes, most churches do offer invitation for salvation at the end of their services, but is there a clear and focused preaching and presentation of the gospel before that?

Compared with other corporations, if the gospel is our core, then we would be out of business. Look at companies that have refused to go where the people are: Radio Shack, Sears, Macy's, and JC Penney. Radio Shack is bankrupt and going out of business. Others are all closing up their physical doors and laying off thousands of employees. They all have one thing in common: They did not have the foresight to go online and market and sell where the people are—in their homes. We must go where they are to tell them the love of Christ. It is no longer sufficient to make the church building the focal point of being and doing church. We must turn our faces outward instead of inward.

The church's greatest resources are the people of God, the body of Christ. We must deploy the body of Christ to work the work of Christ. Many people are unemployed and underemployed by their church—in their use of talents for the work of the ministry that starts in the church and goes outside to wherever God's people are placed. The talents are just sitting, collecting dust. Maybe it is a reflection of our priorities and how the church uses its funds. We use most of our financial resources for ourselves. Look at the summary of a study compiled by the *Evangelical Christian Credit Union,* titled "Investing in Ministries":

A study done by the Evangelical Christian Credit Union shows that churches spend 83% of their budget on administrative expenses and only about 5% on charitable programs. This is a completely astounding disparity from how any charity should operate. Any other charity in the world would be considered grossly inefficient and even negligent with that kind of distribution of their budget.

The majority of the 83 percent (this is conservative; some studies cite up to 95 percent) is spent on salaries, building expenses, and church programs that benefit the members. The numbers speak for themselves and confirm an inward-focused church.

Most churches have so many weekly programs focused on members that if an average family attended them all, they would be exhausted and worn out. They would spend most of their time in the church building, while at the same time, they would not know their next-door neighbors. No wonder people sit in churches for years without any real passion for the things of God but just come each Sunday to be soothed of their past wounds.

Is the church doing some good? Yes. But are we doing what we are supposed to be doing? Why are we so self-absorbed and consumed with ourselves instead of living for the One who died for us? That is the focus of this assessment of the state of the church. Let's continue the assessment as we zero in on missionary efforts and individual and corporate evangelism.

The Evangelism Club vs. Witnesses

We have relegated evangelism to a very few and to members of the soul-winners clubs. Look at a typical announcement in a church bulletin, which reads something like this: "There will be a 12-week class on evangelism for those who want to join the Evangelism Club. There will be opportunities for hands-on practical training and outreach. Please contact so-and-so if you are interested. There is a $20 cost for the book and material for the training." We recognize and applaud all efforts toward evangelism. As Paul said, even when the gospel is preached out of selfish motives (see Philippians 1:15), at least it is being preached and he is happy and rejoices. But when did the Great Commission to the church become a commission to the "club" and not the entire church? It has become a multiple choice and a selection on the church cafeteria-style menu. (If you like evangelism, choose items B and C.) We are all baptized with the Holy Spirit to be witnesses (see Acts 1:8).

Our mission flows from the same mission as Christ Jesus. We all have been anointed for the same purpose: "The Spirit of the LORD is upon Me, because He has anointed Me to preach the gospel to the poor; He has sent Me to heal the brokenhearted, To proclaim liberty to the captives, and recovery of sight to the blind, To set at liberty those who are oppressed" (Luke 4:18).

Great things are happening in missionary work. God has been able to use the few who are willing to risk so much to reach people all over the world. America and the rest of the West have been on the forefront of the sending out and the support for foreign missions. The "other world" countries are beginning to do the sending too. We rejoice and thank God.

But there is more to missions that needs our consideration as illustrated by the following:

A Deep-sea Fishing Story

There was a village whose main livelihood was fishing. The waters around them were dangerous. The village would send a few brave fishermen to the deep sea to catch fish. Due to unforeseen circumstances and changes in weather patterns, the same fish they used to spend so much on (time, money, risk of dangerous water, etc.) catching were now swimming near the shore. What did the villagers do? They debated among themselves why the fish near the shore may not be as good as those caught in the deep waters. They totally ignored the shoreline fish and chose to continue spending a lot to send a few fishermen to the deep sea to catch the same fish. Of course, these deep-sea fishermen would never catch as much compared to what the entire village could catch in the shallow waters by the shore.

Though it was a fishing village, most of the villagers had never stepped into the water. The few who did do so once in a while saw it as recreation and only caught a few fish in order to tell stories about them from time to time.

The fishing villagers would also gather once a year to clap for and celebrate the few brave deep-sea fishermen. The deep-sea fishermen and women would tell their exciting stories of exploits. The villagers loved and craved for more of those stories. The village was very satisfied with their deep-sea efforts that were done by the few. In fact, they bragged about the budget set aside for the deep-sea fishing.

Surely you get my point. Should we continue foreign missionary work especially in the unreached places and to the *ethnos* of the world? Absolutely yes. However, we can join in the local missionary work, especially in the West where immigration and migration have brought so many people to our doorsteps. Many missionaries in the Middle East do not have as much liberty to speak to Muslims, such as in countries like Saudi Arabia. But we can speak to any Muslim here in America or Europe without fear of deportation or even of being killed for trying to convert a Muslim to Christ.

We pray that the church will continue to commit to reach the unreached peoples of the world, especially in the so-called 10-40 window. These are mostly Muslims, Hindus, Buddhists and the tribal peoples of the world. I believe that as individuals are trained and participate in corporate evangelism, they will be inspired and quickened by the Holy Spirit to go into foreign missions to reach the unreached.

Individual Friendship Evangelism

How are we doing at the individual level with telling people about Jesus and presenting a clear and comprehensive gospel? I am sorry to say that it is not so good. Some of us have never opened our mouths to tell someone else about the gospel since we believed. Some who have done so before may go for a whole year without intentionally telling someone about Jesus. I have been there and have many friends and church folks who are in the same place right now. How can we live from week to week, month to month, year after year without opening our mouths to say anything to anyone about Christ? It is incomprehensible.

As I said earlier, Stoyan Zaimov, reporting in *The Christian Post* on a new study released in December 2017, wrote, "The percentage of born-again Christians in America continues to decline, a major religious survey has found. And only a minority of the faithful believe they have a strong personal responsibility to share the Gospel."

Zaimov quoted Barna, who had said, "Christianity in America is going through a time of substantial challenge. The Church at-large is not likely to grow in the future unless some fundamental changes in practice are made." He added, "Fewer churches emphasize and equip people for evangelism these days, and the results are obvious and undeniable. The implications of ignoring gospel outreach—especially among children, who are the most receptive audience to the Gospel—are enormous. All the 'church growth' strategies in the world cannot compensate for the absence of an authentic transmission of the good news of what Jesus Christ has done for humanity."

I wholeheartedly agree that drastic "fundamental changes in practice" need to be made and that is what is being proposed in this book. Zaimov continues:

> The results, drawn from a monthly nationwide survey this year that in total interviewed 9,273 American adults, found that just 31 percent of adults identify as born again, following a trend of decline since 2010 . . . The researchers believe that the decline in born-again Christians is largely due to attitudes toward evangelism and salvation. Only 21 percent of adults affirm that they have a strong personal responsibility to share the Gospel with people who hold different views. Among born-again Christ followers, 39 percent agree.

This report is alarming and reflects truly where we are as a church universal.

Can we be real with one another? Many are living out their witness to Jesus, but the majority are not and it is not even on their radar. The average Christian is mostly concerned about his/her welfare and family. Our daily prayers reflect this. When was the last time we prayed for a specific person to hear and receive the truth of the gospel? What about intentional friendship evangelism within our work places, schools, homes and neighborhoods? We are encouraged to do so to get to know people and eventually share the truth of the gospel with them.

Again, few are intentional about this. At best, a few will mention to friends from time to time, "Hey, Jesus loves you." That is good but not enough to save anyone without the presentation of the gospel at some point. There will never be a convenient time to share the gospel with a friend. We must intentionally break the ice with such questions as, "Where are you on your spiritual journey?" or "What is the most important thing to you in this life, and why?" Friendship evangelism is a good idea, but we must at some point explain the gospel to them; otherwise we will end up having cookouts and games with people while they end up heading to hell.

Why are we where we are on individual evangelism? I don't know all the answers. The Lord knows and He is doing something about it. We are not being effective because we have not seen it modeled and we have not practiced it in the community of believers. The church and the pastors must make it the priority from the pulpit. People want to see their pastors engage in evangelism and not just talk about it. As the collective church goes from door to door, people will see results and will be encouraged to be bold to do the same on their own at the one-on-one level.

Also, the joy of the Lord is lacking in most believers, so there is no motivation to speak to people. There is no greater joy than telling someone about the gospel and seeing a new life in Christ formed and come to life. I have never seen anyone who is not filled with great joy at seeing a new born baby. Most times, we come home from church motivated to deal with our issues because of the sermon, but that's not real motivation because it is all focused on ourselves and not on reaching the lost. Until we start living for something bigger than our problems, we will not start living and our joy will not be complete. When we become outward focused and heaven focused (see Colossians 3:1-4), we will forget our problems because they will pale compared to the number of people in eternity without God's presence. Absence of God in any life is the definition of hell. We should not wish hell for anyone, not even our worst enemies.

I would like to make it very clear that there are many outreach efforts going on in various churches and para-church organizations and by individuals. All should continue and are applauded. All I am proposing in this book is to focus and give intentional priority to the preaching of the gospel by all churches and all individual followers of Christ. For example, there is an international students ministry in most American college cities. I was a beneficiary of such a ministry many years ago as a student from Nigeria in Milwaukee, Wisconsin. We have the same organizations in the Washington, DC, area where we now live. Many churches in the area get involved and provide food for the students on Friday nights. The students gather to eat and learn from one another and from host families from the churches. Organizations such Bridge International and International Students Incorporated (ISI), and many other campus ministries, do a good job of coordinating the events and presenting the gospel. There is always a need for volunteers for various tasks regarding the food or for being available to converse with the students. There is the need for volunteers to host the international students during holidays such as Thanksgiving and Christmas with the intention of sharing the gospel with the students.

This Thanksgiving, we hosted four students from India and China. What a joy to have the students spend half the day with us! Our children were excited to have their company. We ate traditional and international food for Thanksgiving. Afterwards we played card games and got to learn more about each other and about our countries. The highlight for me was when, at the end, two of the students stayed much longer and one of them opened up to ask questions about God, Christianity and religion. One of the students was from India and the other was from China. I had asked an open-ended question to them to share their religious or faith experiences growing up. The Indian student is a believer and follower of Christ. The Chinese student was very frank and said he did not grow up with the concept of God like many Chinese people. He was not taught to believe in anything. While in college in China for university undergraduate studies, he met a Chinese Christian girl and they became friends. However, the girl's parents told him that they could not marry because he is not a Christian and that marriage is a triangular relationship with the two at the base and God on top. It was very profound and I was impressed by his understanding. From his expressions, I could see that his heart was broken and that God had been working on him before he arrived in the United States less than three months ago. He now had the opportunity to ask all kinds of questions to learn more about Christianity.

We explained the gospel to him, going back to the basics of who God is and His creation of all people. He agreed that there must be a creator and that it could not have been some big bang. He acknowledged that it was hard for him to believe and come to faith because he couldn't comprehend all of it. I agreed with him and told him that even though I was raised in a church-going Christian family, I did not understand it either, that it wasn't until I was 17 that I heard a clear gospel presentation. It was then that I put my faith and trust in Christ.

He said that something was blocking him from understanding Christianity. We know from Scripture that Satan blinds people's eyes to see the truth of the gospel. I explained that actually what he needed was a relationship with God, his creator. We encouraged him to keep seeking and God would open his eyes to Christ the Savior. We could see his hunger and desire to know the truth of Christ. We suggested to him that God may have brought him to America for the purpose of knowing Christ and being saved. We will continue to pray and follow up with this student. I thank God for him. Please pray for "Brad," which is what we're calling him.

There are so many opportunities like this to reach international students and/or other foreigners anywhere you live. We just have to be intentional and look for such opportunities. I did not have to travel to China and India to be a missionary. I thank God for those who do and are called to do so. God has graciously brought the world to us in the Washington, DC, metro area and I am sure in your area wherever you may live. Let us look for them. They are our neighbors and international students in our colleges and universities.

As we assess the state of the Church, and if we accept the assessment that we must do something with our knowledge and present truth, then hope is not lost. The message of Christ is always redemptive, both for the unbelieving and also for the Church. We see it all over Scripture. For example, Ruth, a Moabite woman, was a descendant of Lot through incest. But she was in the lineage of Christ as the great-grandmother of King David.

There is no reason why we, as a corporate church body, can't use at least one Sunday a month to accomplish the most important mission of the Church: to preach the gospel and make disciples. Is there anything (theologically or biblically) that stops us? I only see one thing: our love for gathering in our church buildings. And that's where we are disobeying God.

4

Warnings and Dangers of Disobedience

" For whom the Lord loveth he chasteneth, and scourgeth every son whom he receiveth. If ye endure chastening, God dealeth with you as with sons; for what son is he whom the father chasteneth not? But if ye be without chastisement, whereof all are partakers, then are ye bastards, and not sons" (Hebrews 12:6-8 KJV).

The state of the church is like a doctor who examines a patient and gives the diagnosis. This chapter is the doctor going further to tell the patient what will happen if the disease is not treated. Our examination tool is the Word of God. The rest of this book will focus on the treatment for the disease.

Scripture is full of warnings and cautions on living this new life in Christ. When we look at 2 Timothy 3:1-5, we have warnings about the last days. We have an enemy who is very busy ensuring that we will have a church full of people "having a form of godliness but denying its power." The apostle Paul wrote Timothy, his spiritual son, and said, "from such people turn away." That is a very strong statement. The incestuous Christianity/Christian is in part what Paul described to Timothy: "lovers of themselves, lovers of money, boasters, proud, without self-control . . . lovers of pleasures rather than lovers of God."

You are probably thinking that Paul is speaking to Timothy about those outside the church. I don't think so. Paul never encouraged his believing readers to keep away from the unbelieving in the world. His heart, like that of Jesus, was to reach the unbelieving. This is clear in 1 Corinthians 5:9-14, where he writes about the so-called brother who was sleeping with his father's wife.

We can see clearly that Scripture does not excuse us to continue in sin or any behavior that is detrimental to our calling to Jesus. The Scriptures are, for that very purpose, "profitable for doctrine, for reproof, for correction, for instruction in righteousness" (2 Timothy 3:16), among other benefits. I would rather take the bitter pill now than suffer later the consequences of an untreated disease. We must "judge those who are inside" (1 Corinthians 5:12) the church.

First, "Examine yourselves to see if you are in the faith; test yourself. Do you not realize that Christ Jesus is in you—unless, of course, you fail the test?" (2 Corinthians 13:5). It does not say, "if you are still in the faith," but rather, "if you are in the faith." Was there faith in Christ from the beginning?

Take Christmas, which I love. Grace, my 9-year-old daughter, did not want to wait, so we decorated right after Thanksgiving. The tree was decorated with ornaments and lights. When night came, a light with different colors was plugged into the outlet to light up the tree and show the beauty of the creation. This is exactly what the Scripture is saying. Are you and I plugged in? As long as the wire is plugged into the power source, light will come. The light and power are coming from the source. Jesus said, "I am the vine and you are the branches and as long as the branch is attached to the vine there will be fruit." There is a relationship.

Plato once said, "An unexamined life is not worth living." It does not matter how many ornaments we have on our tree. When darkness comes (and it will come), if our wires are not plugged into the source, there will be no light. Our life now is like the day, whereas the night will surely come when we die. We must be plugged into Christ while it's day, otherwise we will be in darkness, forever separated from God. That is the definition of hell. When the wire is plugged in, the power comes on and shines and all see the light. When we are in Christ, the light must shine.

We have been lied to and have bought into the idea that we are going to live here on Earth forever. The improvements and advancements in science and technology give us the false impression that we are here for a long time. We never stop to think about the end of life, and it never dawns on us that we could die soon. We pray prayers that make it seem as though we will never die. We rebuke death as if it is ours to decide. The result of such a mentality is that we never believe and reflect on the Scripture that says, "Teach us to number our days, that we may gain a heart of wisdom" (Psalm 90:12).

As such, we never take God's commands seriously because we think we have all the time in the world to get to it someday. "Go and make disciples" is one of those commands that are in our bucket of "someday." Someday could be today for us to die. This is a hard truth.

We just lost a very young friend, which brings this truth very home and near to me. Lord, help us to number our days. "Show me, LORD, my life's end and the number of my days; let me know how fleeting my life is" (Psalm 39:4). Jesus said, "As long as it is day, we must do the works of him who sent me. Night is coming, when no one can work." We must have the same attitude as Christ when it comes to doing the will of our Father God.

Jesus said by their fruits you shall know them. Don't tell me we are saved by grace when we do not produce the fruits of grace and the deeds empowered by the grace of God. The writer of Hebrews is even more blunt: "For the earth which drinks in the rain that often comes upon it, and bears herbs useful for those by whom it is cultivated, receives blessing from God; but if it bears thorns and briers, it is rejected and near to being cursed, whose end is to be burned" (Hebrews 6:7-8). We must produce the desired and designed fruit of the Holy Spirit for which God has blessed us and filled us with His Spirit.

Is it possible that we have tested the goodness of God and not produced that goodness? There is only one goodness in us and that is Jesus the good Shepherd and the righteous one who has filled us with Himself, the Holy Spirit. For we cannot say that Jesus is Lord without the Holy Spirit speaking through us.

Friends, making disciples is not a suggestion. It is the proof of who we are in Christ. We have Christ and Christ is in us; and we don't have the choice to make disciples. How do we think the Lord added to the church daily those who lived in the book of Acts? The disciples were making other disciples corporately and individually. This new life we now live is not us who live but Christ living in us. It is not about us; it's all about Christ. It is not about self-absorption and self-gratification in our incestuous, sinful lifestyle. I believe the Holy Spirit is sending us clear warnings.

Can we look beyond where we are today to the very end of our lives? Who do we think Jesus is speaking about when He said, "Depart from Me" (Matthew 7:21-33)? It seems very clear that He is speaking to some people in present, past and future church congregations. I am never saying that evangelism is the basis of our salvation, nor do I wish to say that going to heaven or hell is determined by one's faithfulness in evangelism. Rather, all I am saying is there must be fruit from our salvation and one of them has to be witnessing for Christ. The Spirit of Christ is the spirit of witness. In Matthew 7:15-20, Jesus was saying that by their fruits we shall know them. My point is for us to examine if we are in the faith first of all. That examination must lead to the Holy Spirit bearing witness with us that we are His children, and hence obedient children to the greatest commission to "go and make disciples." We should not pretend to ignore the fact that some in our churches are not saved, and if they remain unsaved, they will hear the words, "I never knew you; depart from Me."

How do you know that you are not one of those? How do I know that I am not one of those? Jesus is using the relationship criteria. There is no better indication of the relationship with the Father apart from the presence of the Holy Spirit in us. If the Holy Spirit is present, there will be fruit of the Spirit and the works of the Spirit. It's all in chapters 14 through 16 of John's Gospel.

Friends, I don't want to shock you, but that's exactly what I intended to do by writing. Jesus said it is a "narrow gate and difficult way" and only a few find it and get through. Are we on the "broad way" where there are many who think making disciples is not for them and only for the "super Christian"? There are no super Christians, only Spirit-filled Christians. Every Spirit-filled Christian is a witness of and for Christ. It is an oxymoron to say one is Spirit-filled and not be a witness and making disciples. Oh, we may be saying that people can just observe us and by osmosis experience Jesus and believe in Him. The Holy Spirit is intentional in declaring the gospel and in making Christ known through the Word. In fact, Jesus is called the Word in John 1. Don't tell me we want someone to know Christ without speaking the word of truth. Jesus also said, "I am the truth," so let us boldly declare Jesus to the whole world.

It is good to do good works. It's been said that there are many ways of being a witness for Christ, and I agree. But do we think that people, by seeing our good works alone, will come to faith in Jesus? People may be drawn to us but we still must tell them the hope we have, which is Christ Jesus Himself. On one hand, we believe that we were saved by God's grace through faith, which comes by hearing the gospel. So how can we turn around and believe that another person will trust in Christ by just seeing our good works, without us preaching Christ crucified to the person?

There is great need for endurance and patience and perseverance to the end. Paul said, "I press on." Paul, the apostle of grace (see Ephesians 2:8), said, "We desire that each one of you show the same diligence to the full assurance of hope until the end, that you do not become sluggish, but imitate those who through faith and patience inherit the promises" (Hebrews 6: 11-12). This is the encouragement for us. But there is no room for laziness.

Accounting and Reckoning

We must give accounting of all the Lord has given us at the individual and corporate levels. Our accounting is not at the judgment seat for condemnation but at the crowning of the saints for God's glory. (see 2 Corinthians 5:10). Pastors, board members, elders and church members must account for congregational resources and for the neighborhood where the church building is located. How did we influence the neighborhood with the people and resources we were given? In Matthew 25:20-30, we read about the servants to whom their master gave various talents to trade. The one with five gained five more and the one with two gained two more.

But what about the wicked servant who hid his talents? He was indeed a servant selected by his master, just as the others. What does it mean to hide and bury the talent? Why is the servant blaming the master? Isn't it what many of us in the church are doing by blaming God? Are we riding on God's sovereignty and taking Him for granted? Oh, He is God and He can save anyone He wants to save, and He does not need us! If He does not need us, then why did He tell us to go and tell the gospel to the world? If the master did not need the servant in this story of Jesus, then why did he give the talent to him to trade with?

We cannot excuse obedience with God's nature. Yes, He is sovereign. But are we taking God and His Word seriously? This servant showed no intention of obeying the master. Rather, he *intentionally* buried the talent. The master was willing to accept even a minimal effort toward obedience, which was to have his money deposited with the bank to earn some interest. The master would have commended the servant for at least that. A modern-day equivalent could be helping and supporting those who are at the forefront, like missionaries. Depositing in the bank may be telling someone about Jesus' death, burial and resurrection, even when we cannot explain all the mystery of the Trinity and other difficult subjects to someone who is yet to hear about Christ. By depositing the minimum of God's Word in someone, it is sure to bear fruit because God will cause it to grow. God will send someone else to water the seed we have sowed and to bring growth and increase.

What was the real offense of the servant who hid the talent? He did not trust his master and took him for granted. The servant said, "I was afraid." Why? There was no trust. Where there is no trust, there is fear. Where there is no love or understanding of God's love, there is fear, for perfect love casts out fear. The "fearful" will not inherit God's kingdom. This servant will not inherit God's kingdom. "And cast the unprofitable servant into the outer darkness. There will be weeping and gnashing of teeth" (Matthew

25:30). May we never forget this truth and may it never be our case, for we have been warned.

How are we intentionally "burying" the gospel in our day? It is a question that must be asked and answered. We must answer it now before it's too late. As with the servants in the story who did not know when their master would return, so too we do not know when our Master will return. In addition, there is a time for everything. This is the time for the harvest for which we did not labor. It's God's harvest field and the people are His harvest. There is a season for harvest corporately and individually for all of us. Our season of harvest is now, while we are living, before we die or Christ comes—whichever comes first. We must use all seasons of our lives for the harvest of souls.

Ashamed of Me and My Gospel

In 2 Timothy 1:8-11, Paul tells Timothy not to be ashamed of the gospel, saying, "For I am not ashamed of the Gospel of Christ, for it is the power of God to salvation for everyone who believes" (Romans 1:16).

Jesus Himself said not to be ashamed of Him: "For whoever is ashamed of Me and My words, of him the Son of Man will be ashamed when He comes in His own glory, and in His Father's and of the holy angels" (Luke 9:23-26).

It cannot be any clearer a warning. If we belong to Christ and are to follow Him, then we must take up our cross and follow. Jesus spelled out the consequences of being ashamed of Him and not talking about Him to others. Commenting on this passage, David Guzik, pastor of Calvary Chapel Santa Barbara, California, said:

> It's no wonder that some were ashamed of Jesus during the days of His earthly ministry; it is astounding that any would be ashamed of Him today . . . Jesus, loving

and praying for His people from heaven. Who could be ashamed of *that*? Yet, some are ashamed. The ashamed man believes; you can't be ashamed of something you don't believe in. He believes but doesn't take satisfaction and confidence in his belief. Ashamed means that you don't want to be seen together in public. Ashamed means that you don't want to talk about Him. Ashamed means that you avoid Him when possible. Some are ashamed out of fear, some out of social pressure, some out of intellectual or cultural pride. Objectively considered, such shame is a strange phenomenon.

We say we are afraid and ashamed to go door to door to tell people about Christ. However, we are the same people who take our children and knock on doors asking for candy and celebrating Halloween, which glorifies a world of darkness. We are the same people who are not ashamed to go door to door to canvass and campaign for our favorite politicians. We will talk to all our friends and relatives nonstop about a presidential candidate, but we cannot open our mouths to mention Jesus and His gospel. We are well informed on every other subject except the gospel. We will read novels of 400 or more pages in a couple of days, but we have not cracked open our Bibles in more than a week or even months. We are the same people who will go door to door to sell products such as Mary Kay, various multi-level or pyramid-scheme businesses, and of course Girl Scout cookies. We will call and befriend anyone so that they buy our products. We are not ashamed to call at any time and interrupt people's dinners and schedules to sell our products and/or to win someone over to our political persuasions.

We can talk about sports all day and sit on the couch most of Saturday and Sunday to watch football or soccer but we don't have any time for telling someone about Jesus or for praying for the unsaved. We will invite, party and watch our Super Bowl or World Cup soccer matches but we cannot invite anyone to our house to hear and celebrate the greatest victory of all time: the victory on the cross. We now spend countless hours on social media, checking, chatting and comparing ourselves to people we know and don't even know. It is said that an average American watches more than five hours of TV daily. That is 33 percent of the average waking time of 15 hours a day. How absurd are these pictures? If we tell our church generation that we don't have it wrong, then we are fooling ourselves. Now is the time we can examine ourselves and tell ourselves the truth, before it is too late. We must work "while it is the day," just like Jesus.

Do the words of Jesus mean anything to us and do they instill reverent fear in us? Will Jesus go through with His promise of being ashamed of those who cannot speak on His behalf and who do not want to be seen with Him in public? There are no closet Christians or followers of Jesus. If we are walking and following someone, then we will go where the person is leading and in the same direction. We will also be seen together with the one we are following. Are we following Jesus? Are we ashamed of Jesus? We must all answer these questions.

Oh, you may now say that I am judging you. Yes and no. I am judging myself and examining myself to see if I am in the faith. If the words of God in this book speak to you, then maybe you can do the same. Examine yourself and see if you are in the faith. Jesus said that if anyone wills, let him/her follow me. He will never force us to do anything against our will. Jesus will never force anyone, not even the first twelve disciples. After some stopped following Him, Jesus turned to the Twelve and asked, "Do you want to leave too?" (John 6:66-67).

In an article in *The Christian Post*, Sheryl Lynn reported, "Fear has been cited as a major reason many Christians don't share their faith with others. But one Southern Baptist says there are many more reasons Christians are reluctant to share the Gospel, including not being real believers."

Chuck Lawless, dean and vice president of Graduate Studies and Ministry Centers at Southeastern Seminary in Wake Forest, North Carolina, has said another reason for the lack of evangelism among Christians is that many are "undiscipled pluralists." "Deep down, they believe there are multiple ways to God," he said, "and no one has intentionally, clearly shown them otherwise from the Scriptures." Other reasons Christians don't evangelize, according to Lawless, include:

- Not knowing many nonbelievers anyway (especially for those who have been in the church for a long time);
- Misapplying biblical teachings and believing there's no reason to evangelize;
- Buying into political correctness—that is, believing that it really is unkind and intolerant to claim there is only one way to God;
- Struggling with their own sin;
- Feeling that life has enough battles of its own and trying to survive another day (evangelism will have to wait). These people are exhausted and beaten up and feel they can't tell a stranger that Christianity works when it hasn't worked for them.

We must repent of our sin of self-absorption, of being out of focus, and of being inwardly focused. Sunday is the most important and most resourceful day for any church. The people are the most important resource of any church. On Sundays, all the people are present. If Sunday is the Lord's day, then let it be His, including the scheduling of services and what the church does with its time on that day. When did it become ours to decide, as if we have rights and entitlements to Sunday? In fact, every day is the Lord's. None belong to us. Why can't we as a corporate church body use Sundays to accomplish the most important mission of the Church: to preach the gospel and make disciples? Why can't I, as an individual follower of Christ, tell people about Jesus and His gospel in my daily contacts and interactions with people? Why should I be ashamed of Jesus Christ, who died for me? Jesus healed people on Sundays. Sunday is a day of rest but not rest from souls of people heading to a forever burning hell.

5

Affirmations of Our Beliefs

'm calling for a major paradigm shift in how we do church. The shift is that we use at least one Sunday a month to go outside to preach the gospel, to pray with people, and to show them we care and that Jesus cares for all people regardless of their sins.

There will be no change in our behavior without a change in belief. What is it that we must believe that will help us change our behavior as individuals and as a corporate body? We are talking about a shift of significant proportion that can be likened to the turning of a big ship in the ocean that is heading for a major shipwreck. But such a turn requires a solid foundation.

Below is my summary of our major beliefs with regards to the mission of Christ and to making disciples. My best way of summarizing, rehearsing, restating and affirming is by asking rhetorical questions that lead us to obvious answers. There is no particular sequence to it. My hope is that we will become sold-out to the truth of the gospel and its power to save the sinner and to reconcile and restore him/her to the Father.

Questions, Answers and Statements We Must Affirm

God is either true or He is not. Jesus is either true or He is not. The Holy Spirit is either true or He is not. The Bible is either true or it is not. Jesus either saves a person from sin and reconciles him to God the Father or He does not. Either a person is saved or he is not. Either a saved person has the spirit of Christ or he does not. Either the Spirit of Christ is alive and active in a saved person or the person does not have the Spirit. The Spirit of Christ is neither lukewarm nor cold. He said He will baptize with fire, not coldness.

The Church is either the bride of Christ or she is not. Either Christ is the head of the Church or He is not. Either the Church embodies the Spirit of Christ or it does not.

The most important thing in a believer's life is Jesus Christ. The most important thing in a church's life is Jesus Christ. Either the gospel is the power of Christ unto salvation or it is not. Either the gospel is the only means of salvation or it is not. Either the gospel is the most important thing in a believer's life or it is not. Either the gospel is the most important thing in a church's life or it is not.

Either Jesus died on the cross, was buried and rose again, or He did not. Either the gospel is Jesus Christ crucified or it is not. Either the gospel is the core business of the Church or it is not.

Either I am saved by believing and trusting Jesus Christ or I am not saved. If I am saved, I am either going to be with God forever or I am not. If someone is not saved, either he/she will be separated from God forever or it is a lie. If I am saved, I am either going to heaven or I am not. If I am not saved, I am either going to hell or I am not. If a person is not saved, I either believe he/she is going to hell or he/she is not. If I truly believe someone is going to hell, I either do something about it or not. If someone is going to hell, either the only person who can save him is Jesus Christ or not. If Jesus can save people, I either tell them about having faith in Jesus or I do not.

I either love Jesus or I don't. If I love Jesus, I either love what He died for or I don't love Him. If I love Jesus, I will either obey His command or I won't. If I don't tell a person about Jesus, I either don't believe in Jesus or that He does not save.

Which is true? Two opposites cannot be true at the same time. Something is either hot or cold. Something is either black or white. Something is either true or false.

Do I truly believe that I was dead and have been made alive in Christ? A corpse can never wake itself up. If I was a corpse and now am alive, why do I think other corpses around me would wake themselves up? Christ alone woke me up and gave me a new life, therefore, only Christ can give new life to others who are yet dead in their trespasses and sin (see Ephesians 2:1-3). Someone said that Jesus did not come to make bad people to become good people. Jesus came to make dead people alive again. Apostle Paul wrote through the inspiration of the Holy Spirit and documented most of the church's key doctrines in the book of Ephesians.

Good Works to Do

According to Paul, we have been saved by the grace of God through faith, which has been given to us. We are not saved by any good works and will never be saved by them. However, we have been given work to do for which we have been "created in Christ Jesus for good works, which God prepared beforehand that we should walk in them" (Ephesians 2:10).

"Good works" is a major belief we must restate and affirm. If God had the intention of only saving us from hell, then He would have called us home immediately after we were saved. God did not do that because He always has in mind the good works we will do. A major good work is to join Him in calling His other children to Himself through our obedience in preaching the gospel. Again, I repeat, preaching the gospel and being a witness for Christ is a product of our salvation and never the basis for our salvation.

As a church and as followers of Christ, do we really believe the truth of the Bible and the doctrines we claim to affirm? That is a question that we must ask ourselves and answer. Christian apologist and evangelist Ravi Zacharias asked the same question when he was speaking on the doctrine of hell and the eternality of hell. He illustrated his point with a very soul-searching story:

> There was an English criminal named Charlie Peace. Charlie was being taken to his execution when he stopped a man, a chaplain, who was callously reading a prepared passage from Scripture.
>
> Charlie asked the man, "Where are you reading from?"
>
> The chaplain said it was the Bible.
>
> He asked, "Chaplain, do you believe it?"
>
> The chaplain said he did.
>
> Charlie asked again, "Do you really believe it?"
>
> The chaplain said, "Yes."
>
> Charlie then said, "Chaplain, sir, if I believed what you and many Christians claim to believe, even one-tenth of what you claim to believe about hell, I would crawl across England on my hands and knees even if it were to be littered

with glass pieces, and I would count it worth my while to save one soul from that hell that you so glibly talk about."

Is this what we believe about hell? What are we doing about it? Some in the church are doing so because they believe that this hell we "glibly talk about" is real. Tom Doyle, a former pastor of a thriving church in America, left everything and moved his family to the Middle East because they heard the voice of God tell them to support God's work in that region. Doyle has documented and compiled for us the faith and courage of former Muslims who truly believe and trust in Jesus Christ in his book *Standing in the Fire: Courageous Christians Living in Frightening Times.* He wrote:

> The people you'll meet in *Standing in the Fire* are believers who have caught on to the devil's strategy and won't fall for it. They've seen the worst his minions can throw at the world, and they are not leaving the scene, no matter how hot the fire gets. Their courage and faith through unthinkable confrontations with radical Islam is inspiring . . . it is a collection of true accounts of courageous Christians facing down the enemies who appear in today's news stories.

I was captivated by all the stories, such as one titled "The Syrian Firing Squad." In this, a man named Osama had a cousin, Jamal, who had miraculously become a follower of Christ. Jamal could no longer hide his faith but had to tell his cousin Osama about it because he loved him so much. The problem was that Osama was the leader of the local ISIS unit. Through Jamal, Osama came to faith in Christ. Soon, other ISIS members found out and started to torture Osama daily. He was asked to renounce Jesus but he refused. Osama was sent to the firing squad but, through a miracle of another changed heart of an ISIS leader, he survived the firing squad as others died around him. Osama escaped and has been ministering to others since then.

If you ever have a chance, please read this book to build your courage and learn how to never run in the face of fear because greater is He that is in us than he that is in the world.

These believers in Christ risk their lives daily to reach others, especially Muslims, with the gospel of Christ. Some have died in the process. Others have said that they cannot stop because they wish to reach their people and give them the only hope there is: Jesus Christ. They believe and affirm the doctrines we have reviewed, and that belief motivates them to do what they do, which is to risk all for Christ.

Stories like these make me wonder how much we, in the West, believe, especially when someone says it is very dangerous to knock on people's doors in America to tell them the good news of the gospel. The real danger is in the Middle East and other parts of the world where people lose their lives to speak about Christ.

Lord, help us learn from them.

Dying in the Church Building

As I wrote this section, there was a very sad and tragic incident that was all over the news in America. On November 5, 2017, an ex-military man walked into First Baptist Church of Sutherland Springs, Texas, and shot and killed 26 people, then himself. Among the dead were the assistant pastor and his wife, along with six members of his family and the senior pastor's daughter. The church secretary was also killed. The church was in a small town where everyone knows almost everyone.

Can this happen anywhere else? Yes. Can it happen to anyone, including any of us? We don't know and neither did all the people in that church know on that fateful Sunday. Many may never experience the tragic end like the one in the Texas church, but death is happening daily and people are leaving Earth without Christ and going into hell, even while in church. Worse, many outside the church have not been presented with the message of the gospel so that they can be awakened to a new life in Christ.

Do You Have a Relationship with God?

Jesus' parable about the ten virgins (see Matthew 25:1-13) said that five of the ten, the "wise virgins," had oil in the lamps, and the other five, the "foolish virgins," did not. When the bridegroom came, only the five wise virgins were allowed into the wedding banquet. Does that hint at the percentage of people in our churches who don't have a relationship with God? If so, why are we not weeping from the pews and the pulpits instead of feeding them with the same old lukewarm messages that will never cause the people to repent and turn to Christ? As ministers, we have come to love our pulpit preaching so much that we are willing to preach the enticing words of men instead of preaching Christ crucified. We have come to love the accolades we receive and the highs we feel from performance. Jesus wept over Jerusalem.

> *Lord, help us to weep for those who sit next to us in church but are still headed to hell. Lord, save these who are in our churches.*

I am reminded of Jesus' parable that speaks about the wheat and the tares, or weeds (see Matthew 13:24-30). The workers wanted to uproot the weeds, but they were told not to do so for the Father will do that at the end. In a farm field, there are usually weeds that come along and that often look like the good crops. My parents did subsistence farming, so I observed that growing up. Is it possible that we are the weed in the midst of the wheat? Or is it possible that we, as the wheat, were sitting next to a person this past Sunday who is a "tare"? Truly, let the judgment begin in the house of God.

Is there still hope for the salvation of the one who does not have a living relationship with Christ and is just warming up the benches on Sundays? Yes. More specifically, is there still time for you, the reader, to enter into an everlasting relationship with Christ if you have never done so before? It is a resounding yes. Paul writes to the young pastor Titus to not give up in his efforts to reach all for Christ, even in the church (see Titus 2:11-15).

Salvation is for all. God has made salvation available for all, including you and me. The one thing that will stop us or anyone in or outside the church from entering into a relationship with Christ right now is pride. That pride speaks too loudly and asks, *What will others think of me after all these years or months of attending church?* It doesn't matter what anyone else thinks about you. What is most important is what God thinks and the truth of His words in your situation. You can start a new life right now. You only need to acknowledge and accept that Christ died for you on the cross and paid for your past, present and future sins to set you free from wickedness and the coming wrath of God. That is why the gospel is called the good news. We do not earn it. Jesus did all the work and heavy lifting on the cross and now He invites you to enter His rest. What else are you waiting for? You and I may not be here tomorrow, for "now" is the day of salvation. If you're unsure of where you stand, please pray the following prayer:

Dear God, I admit that I am a sinner and need Your forgiveness. I repent and ask that You forgive me my sins. I accept You, Jesus Christ, as my Lord and Savior, who gave Your life for my sins. I entrust my life to You, Father God. Please come into my life and help me live a life that pleases You, denying ungodliness and worldly lusts, and living soberly, righteously, and godly in the present age. Fill me with Your Holy Spirit to live this new life of Christ in me. Amen.

Congratulations! The Bible says that you are now a child of God (see John 1:12) because you now believe and trust Jesus. You are also a new creation in Christ and the old has gone (see 2 Corinthians 5:16-21). You have been given a new nature, a spiritual nature, because now the spirit of Christ, the Holy Spirit, lives in you. If God now lives in you, the life you will live going forward forever will be God living through you. It is impossible to live any life that pleases God except Christ living in you. Now go ahead and tell someone and the whole world that Christ now lives in you and that you are a brand-new person and a child of God. Do not be ashamed of following Christ.

Now you can read the rest of this book with joy and put it into practice, telling people about Jesus and calling them to put their faith and trust in Jesus for all He has done on the cross for all to be saved. This is the gospel, the good news that all your sins and my sins are forgiven forever and now we can live in gratitude to Christ for the rest of our lives. We are now eager to do good works not for salvation but because we have been saved from hell. This calls for great rejoicing, so let us go ahead and shout and praise God.

The beliefs and affirmations we have reviewed in this section should anchor us to a major shift in the way we do church and be church. There is one more core belief we will consider in the next chapter. We believe that *we* are the temple of the Holy Spirit. When we are not convinced of this truth, we can place unnecessary emphasis on the physical building we often refer to as the church. That sometimes become a hindrance to fulfilling the gospel mission.

6

Trapped in the Building

Scripture says, "Do you not know that your bodies are the temple of the Holy Spirit, who is in you, whom you have received from God?" (1 Corinthians 6:19). I understand this to mean that the Holy Spirit dwells in me and that He is the Spirit of Christ who now lives in me. As such, every believer and follower of Christ has the Spirit of Christ living in them 24/7. The presence of God is now with us, and the scripture in Hebrews 13:5 that says "I will never leave you nor forsake you" has been made a living truth. Jesus Himself promised us, "Surely I am with you always, to the very end of the age." We are no longer limited by physical location and circumstances to experience and worship our God who lives in us. This is a very liberating truth, and whom the Son sets free is free indeed.

The presence of the Holy Spirit is a present reality; at the same time, we are collectively being built into a holy temple for the dwelling of God (see Ephesians 2:19-22).

So, what does being a temple of God have to do with fulfilling our call to the Great Commission, which is making disciples? It is my assessment that we have confused the importance of the physical building with the real housing of God; that is, *we* are the temple of the Holy Spirit. All true followers/believers in Christ are the temple of God. The physical church building is important, but it is not a substitute for the presence of God in believers. Of course, our God is omnipresent and therefore dwells in all the Earth. Our God is not more present in the church building than He is present in us in our various houses and homes.

Implicit in the order to "go and make disciples" is the truth that as we go, Jesus has gone before us and will transform people wherever we meet them. The requirement was not to bring people to a temple or church building for them to encounter Jesus and be transformed by Him. How did we then become building-focused and trapped in the building?

How Did We Get Where We Are Now?

Ever since the big cathedrals were built hundreds of years ago and became the focal point of worship, the church DNA has changed. We became building-focused instead of outward-focused. We expect people to come to our church to experience God as if Christ is limited to the building. Going out to tell people that Jesus loves them is no longer the measure of joy and success. Rather, the size and completion of the church building have become the joys and pride of most, if not all congregations. Once the building is finished, we feel a false sense of great accomplishment and go into our church comfort nests.

Look at where the cars are parked in your neighborhood as you go to your church building and realize that where you are heading is not the hottest thing in town on Sunday morning. People are definitely in their homes. They are not itching and craving to drive to some building on Sunday morning, and why should they? We must change from a building focus to a people focus. We can't bring people to become like us in the building and make them slaves of the building.

It's time to take a second look and redefine what the purpose is of our gathering in a building. Do we have to gather? Yes, but how often and for what purpose? How do our gatherings in a building hinder or help reaching outward to seek and save the lost? We cannot continue in the same building-focused business as usual and expect a new and different result. Doing the same thing over and over and expecting a different result is crazy.

Our buildings have made us feel "rich and lacking nothing" and "lukewarm." In his *Time of Grace* television broadcast, the Reverend Mark Jeske, pastor of St. Marcus Lutheran Church in Milwaukee, Wisconsin, calls the church building our "clubhouse." How did the church get to be so lukewarm, neither hot nor cold? Jesus foresaw it and had much to say about it in Revelation 3:14-19, His love letter to the Laodicean church. "I correct and discipline everyone I love. So be diligent and turn from your indifference," He said.

Where do we go from here? We must repent and become hot—hot for Jesus, hot for His gospel, hot for loving one another, and hot for reaching the world for Jesus. We must also be cold like a refreshing water to welcome the bruised to comfort them and be drink for the thirsty. We must collectively do something. We must not be lukewarm.

The Army in the Barracks
No army exists only in the barracks or the base. Every army uses the barracks as a temporary dwelling and deploys its soldiers

outside the base for war. The fight cannot be fought in the barracks, nor do you invite invading nations into the base for conflict engagement. When you win the war outside, you bring the captured and the surrendered back to the base, along with the spoils of war.

The church cannot be any different. We are soldiers of the cross and in warfare. The battle must be fought outside the church building and we must get out of our church-building-base mentality for deployment. Remember, the battle is already won and we are "more than conquerors." And "thanks be to God, who gives us the victory through our Lord Jesus Christ" (1 Corinthians 15:57). We are riding on Christ's victory and He gives us triumph always. We may have some fears about witnessing, but the Holy Spirit is always with us, even when we are slammed in the process. God has already prepared the people outside the church building. They are just waiting for us to show up.

Let us continue to examine ourselves. We have become like a nice sports car that stays parked in the garage. We clean and polish it each Sunday. We check the oil and top off all vital fluids. We brag about how our car is in top shape, then never pull it out of the garage to drive on the road. Our neighbors only see the car on Sunday when we open the garage to again clean, wax and polish it. Occasionally we will invite top mechanics to come do serious work on the car while still in the garage. The mechanic will often recommend upgrading to a bigger engine and will give us additives to mix with the fuel to gain better performance on the road.

So, what good is our car? At this point we may call it a car but is it really a car if never driven? I'd call it a form of godliness and denying the power thereof. Even antique cars get to be driven once or twice a year for car shows. At least they get out of the garage and onto the road. Our cars have never gone out, or perhaps they went on the road a long time ago. We have never given anyone a ride in our car. For all practical purposes, our sports car is really not a car, though it has everything a car may have. It has not fulfilled the purpose for which the car designer and maker intended. Someday, the car will be assigned to the junkyard for not fulfilling its purpose. We can never blame the car maker because the choice is ours to pull the car from the garage and drive everywhere for the intended purpose.

Three Tabernacles

I love the apostle Peter. He is always our test case and we learn so much from his mistakes. Growth is not absence of mistakes but learning from our mistakes and those of others. Peter again tries to hold Jesus ransom by his preconceived ideas of who Jesus is and what He should be doing and where He should be doing it. We are doing the same today. My opinion and yours do not change who God our Father, His Son Jesus Christ, and His Holy Spirit is. God will remain forever God and in control and in charge of the world He created. No liberal or conservative thinking or ideology can change that.

So, look at what Peter said during the transfiguration of Jesus on the mountain: "Lord, it is good for us to be here; if You wish, let us make here three tabernacles: one for You, one for Moses, and one for Elijah" (Matthew 17:4).

In other words: "Hey, Jesus, let's just hang out here; forget about everyone else and forget about Your sole mission on Earth. Let's erect our great buildings and cathedrals to hang out, just us Christians with our Jesus." That is not going to happen, Peter. The Father quickly rebukes Peter just as Jesus had rebuked him a few days prior when He told Peter, "Get behind Me, Satan! You are an offense to Me, for you are not mindful of the things of God, but the things of men" (Matthew 16:23). Then on the Mount of Transfiguration, "While he was still speaking, behold, a bright cloud overshadowed them; and suddenly a voice came out of the cloud, saying, 'This is My Beloved Son, in whom I am well pleased.

Hear Him!'" (Matthew 17:5). God the Father spoke directly to Peter, saying, in effect, "Cut it out, Peter, and listen to my beloved Son, Jesus."

Do we "hear Him" or are we hearing ourselves in all that is going on around us, even in good things such as great church fellowship? The voice of God through His Word and the whispers of His Holy Spirit in our hearts are the only things we need to hear. Let's stop listening to everyone else but God. God will not confuse us, but we and others will confuse us.

Jesus had to go to the cross, and nothing was going to stop Him. Our salvation was at stake and was not to be traded for good times on the Mount of Transfiguration as Peter suggested. Like Jesus, we must come down to the valley where the people who really need salvation are. We cannot stay on our church-building mountain, or in our Bible study, retreat and conference mountains, and refuse to get to the neighbors and communities that need us and our Jesus.

Saints, let's go do what we have heard. Let's pray for someone today and tell them about the good news of salvation, which is in Christ's death and resurrection alone. Let's make that phone call, write that letter, forgive that one who has hurt us so badly. Yesterday is gone. We can start again today just like the disciples. Fear of what people will say and the shame of past failure will cripple us from doing what we need to do.

Jesus is always there to jump-start us again when we miss it. Still at the Mount of Transfiguration, "Jesus came and touched them [the disciples Peter, James and John] and said, 'Arise, and do not be afraid.' When they had lifted up their eyes, they saw no one but Jesus only" (Matthew 17:7-8). May we see only Jesus today when we rise from our past mistakes. May God's grace be sufficient for us as we determine to obey Him in and outside the church building.

Bearing Shame Outside the Camp

You don't find something until you start looking and paying attention. My eyes and heart caught the words in the Bible where the writer of Hebrews—by the Holy Spirit—encourages us to bear shame and reproach outside the camp, just as Jesus did (see Hebrews 13:12-16). There is no hiding inside the camp if we are following Jesus and are to be known as His disciples.

In the context of this concluding chapter of Hebrews, we are encouraged to press on to the very end through faith and endurance. We are to "openly profess His name" as a fruit and sacrifice of praise. To me, it means going out to preach His gospels with words and sharing with others the wonderful things accomplished by the blood of Jesus.

So, can we be un-trapped from the church-building focus? Yes, we can and we must be un-trapped. We must see the church building as just a tool to get the work done. As with any tool, it must be used properly for the intended purpose. The pastors, deacons or elders/trustees are not custodians and guardians of just a physical building. They are guardians and overseers of the people of God, who are the real temple of God. We must repent for our pride in the physical building and our bragging rights in nice edifices. The sign of repentance would be when we start sending people *out* of the building to go where the people are to reach them with the gospel. Let's use at least one Sunday a month to leave the church building and go to our neighbors to share the gospel of Christ.

I have seen and listened to many pastors encourage their congregations to be witnesses for Christ and the people nod in agreement. The pastors will often repeat the same admonitions from time to time since most people seem not to be heeding them. God's people need the practical examples to do what you are asking them to do. Dear pastors, please lead the people by going out to your neighbors at least one Sunday a month. With God's help, you will see the desired result of flourishing disciple-makers.

There are other turnings and repenting we need to do to be able to make the major paradigm shift being proposed in this book. Let's do business with the Holy Spirit for transformation.

7

The Turn-Around

What are we turning around from and to? The implication of a turn-around is that when one turns around, he or she is no longer facing in the same direction. Someone who has turned around sees new things or the same things from a different angle. We have been self-absorbed, out of focus, and inwardly focused. As we turn around, we will be focused and outwardly focused. We will start seeing differently from what we used to see. We used to see ourselves all the time, but now we will see and focus on who we are supposed to see: our Jesus, and the world He died for. The beauty of repentance is a new beginning, a new perspective, and a new vision.

The good news is that Jesus foresaw where we are today and that is why He spoke about us as a church. He wants us to change, and at the same time He encourages us regarding the things we are doing well. Hope is not lost.

What is it we (the church corporately and as individuals) did at first, and how did we show Him our love? Simply, we loved Him very much, we obeyed, and we preached Christ crucified to all. The word is still "go and make disciples."

Our Lord loves us so much and He is always encouraging us. In Revelation 2:1-7, He tells the Ephesian church and us, "I have seen your hard work and your patient endurance. I know you don't tolerate evil people . . . You have patiently suffered for me without quitting." Who would not like to hear those words? Remember this church? This is the church that the apostle Paul wrote to. You can learn more about the Ephesians by reading Paul's epistle. This church was on fire for Jesus. How did they get to losing their first love and fire? Like us, they became very busy, out of focus, and inwardly focused. You can still be out of focus even while you are suffering for Christ. Once our focus is on what we can do for ourselves, we lose our absolute trust and dependence on Jesus. It is hard to hear someone at whom you are not looking during a conversation. You have to hear, listen and understand in order to obey and do what you are hearing.

In addition, notice that the love for Jesus includes the love for His bride, the church. "You don't love me or each other as you did at first!" Imagine if someone came to your house and said that he was your friend, that he loved you very much, but he wouldn't talk to your wife or be nice to her and didn't care about her. What do you think you would do and say to this pseudo friend? "Get lost and out of my face and out of my house," you would say. "You really don't love me, because my wife and I are one."

How are we treating one another before we even go out to tell people about Jesus and that we love Him? Evangelism can become an annoying noise if we don't love and care for one another in the church. "Though I speak with the tongues of men and of angels, but have not love, I have become sounding brass or a clanging cymbal" (1 Corinthians 13:1). How can we pair up two by two and go door to door to preach the gospel if we don't even care for the one with whom we are paired up?

There is a caveat to Jesus' invitation to turn around and repent. The key is as follows: "Anyone with ears to hear must listen to the Spirit and understand what He is saying to the churches." Can we so far say that we have heard the voice of God through His Word and His Spirit? Do we understand what the Lord is saying to the church of our day? What is He saying to us?

Our Love Story

I remember when I met my wife for the first time. In 1989, my mother passed away. I was living in the U.S., but I traveled back to Nigeria for the funeral and stayed for about two weeks. During this period, my cousin introduced me to a lovely, gorgeous lady. She was a lecturer with my cousin at a local university. All my cousin told me was that "she loves Jesus just like you and talks your language." By the way, my cousin was not at that time fully committed to Christ (thank God, he is now).

He also told me that her name is Udo. Right there, I told him that no way was I going to meet her. What if I liked her? (Our first names are the same: *Udo*, meaning "peace" in the Ibo language.) I fell madly in love with UD, which is what we both agreed that people should call her for differentiation. Then I flew back to America.

We started corresponding by mail and phone. I was so excited that wherever I went, I carried UD's photo to show everyone, whether they asked for it or not. I talked about her nonstop. After six months, I proposed to her via overseas phone call. We eventually got married a year later. Because of my immigration status at that time, I had to wait another year before UD could join me in the States. I so longed for my bride and ceaselessly called, wrote letters, and did whatever was possible, including sending messages through people traveling to Nigeria. I was totally crazy to see her again and never stopped talking about her and showing off the wedding ring to announce to other ladies that I was already taken.

This is my paraphrase of what Jesus is saying in Revelation 2 to the church at Ephesus:

You were madly in love with Me and you told everyone about it. What has happened? Yes, you are busy doing many things in My name, but you have forgotten your first love. Remember how you felt about Me and what I meant to you and turn around and do what you did in the first time; yearn for Me and tell everyone about Me. You yearned to hear from Me through my letters (in the Bible). You talked with Me. Now go back and do these same things again. Don't stop pouring through My Word and don't stop pouring out your heart to Me by talking to Me at all times. Go tell everyone that I, Jesus, am madly in love with you and will love them too if they open their hearts to Me, Jesus.

This is what the Lord has been saying to me about this issue:

You have been on this mountain too long. It's a mountain of soaking and enjoying worship and singing and taking care of yourself and self-pity, of learning and knowledge and classes and conferences. It's time to come down to the valley where the people are. They can't hear you at the top of the mountain because you are too far from them and from the reality of impending death in the valley. I have been equipping you all these years for such a time as this. Use all the training and skills that you already have for doing my business. As for the pastors, yes, you have worked hard, but now get up and finish the work like the faithful and wise servants that have been put in charge.

Fruit of Godly Sorrow

All genuine repentance results in a change in behavior. It is not sufficient to feel goose bumps/sorrow and still do nothing. This is how the apostle Paul admonished and encouraged the Corinthian church: "For godly sorrow produces repentance leading to salvation, not to be regretted; but the sorrow of the world produces death" (2 Corinthians 7:10).

Let's do as the Corinthians did, with diligence, vehement desire, and zeal. Let's take action that proves our repentance.

Lord, we repent of our incestuous Christianity. Please forgive our sins. Forgive us for our nonchalant and careless attitude toward You, our Lord. We have taken You and Your Word for granted. Forgive us for the misuse of precious time and resources You have given us. Forgive us for the misuse of the pulpit platform and for having not made the gospel a priority for the church. We repent of living only for ourselves, and we repent of how we have treated one another without love. Now we turn our hearts to You, our true lover, Jesus Christ. We repent for looking down on people made in Your image and for refusing to see them as sinners needing a savior, just like us.

We thank You, Lord, for forgiving us, and we rest in the assurance of Your Word that says, "If we confess our sins, He is faithful and just and will forgive us our sins and purify us from all unrighteousness" (1 John 1:9). Renew Your right spirit within us and cause us to yearn earnestly for You. Conform us to Your likeness, even at all cost. We surrender to Your rule and governance over our lives, desires and aspirations. May Your will be done in our lives and in the life of Your church. Amen.

Now, let's be bold! Let's go for the drastic turn-around and make the biggest paradigm shift in recent times for the church with the strength of Christ. Let's look at the plan of action in the next chapter and take the gospel from door to door and from person to person. Let's corporately do it at least one Sunday a month for the glory of God. And let's be motivated as followers of Christ to own it as our responsibility to share the gospel with joy wherever we live and in whatever we do in our vocations.

8

The Simple Plan:
Old but New

I f we are going to go from incestuous Christianity to making disciples, we must have a roadmap and plan. We have agreed that our present church condition is inappropriate and cannot be sustained. We have repented of our sins of self-absorption and being lukewarm and are willing to return to our first love, Jesus Christ. Our hearts are being changed and renewed by the Holy Spirit. We now need to "do the things we did at first."

I propose that we use at least one Sunday in a month to go out into our communities to tell them about the love of Christ. It will take the boldness of the Holy Spirit to do this, to depart from the norm, to be radical disciples and radical congregations. We have gathered too long every Sunday to feed and take care of ourselves. We have become an incestuous church just doing inbreeding—that is, people moving from one congregation to another. There's no real growth from outside the camp.

What I envision is a Sunday morning when we spend the first thirty minutes to gather, pray, collect the offering, and give instructions and directions for going out. It will involve everyone except younger kids. Anyone who does not want to go can stay at the church building to pray for us. Everyone is needed in this harvest and so those staying behind and praying are equally as important as those going out. We cannot win this race without fervent prayers.

It is a war and we must lay out the war plan. We will obtain neighborhood maps and appoint leaders to go with groups of two to various neighborhoods. We will check off where we have been, then go to another neighborhood another Sunday. The outreach will be from about 90 minutes to two hours, and then people can come back and pick up their kids from the church building. Everyone is key in this mission. Those staying back and teaching the children are very relevant to the others' success and should never be seen as less important. There should never be any shaming or looking down on those who are not able to go out onto the streets.

The next Sunday can be used to teach any new believers, report results to the congregation, and let people be encouraged. Then we do it again the next month, using another Sunday. I believe that we will get so used to it and encouraged by the results of the harvest that one Sunday a month may not satisfy us any longer and we will be doing more Sundays whenever possible.

Imagine all churches in America and the world giving up just one Sunday for doing what Jesus did with His disciples: sending them out two by two. I call this the "wave" effect. We start from the neighbors nearest to the church building. As we move farther from the church, we cover more ground and more people. At the same time, another nearby church is doing the same thing and moving outward. Sooner or later, the two churches and other churches will have covered and reached their communities for Christ. It will be as the Scripture says: The glory of the Lord will spread all over the Earth as the water covers the sea. Now we can collaborate with other churches in our area to see where they have covered. We will no longer be in competition with one another.

Reaching the world for Christ is now possible and in sight, so let's dream big, take baby and big steps, and see the Lord do what He has always intended: that His gospel be preached to all the world.

Let's give up the pews and the pulpits and the sermonizing just for one Sunday and do the real work for Jesus. Is there any pastor and congregation "crazy" enough for Jesus who would take this bold step to break from the norm?

When we go out, we are not necessarily going out to invite people to our church building and cathedral. We will knock on doors and invite people to Jesus. We will say, "We are your neighbors from the local church. Is there something we can pray with you for? Jesus loves you and died for your sins so that you can experience true life in God." Let people meet Jesus and experience Christ before anything else. Remember, we are not going out to people to necessarily "close the deal" and have them say the sinner's prayer. If they get to that point, we will thank God. We are there to be a chain in the link of what God is already doing in their lives. Let's sow the new seeds and/or water seeds others have already sown. Let God bring the germination and the growth, for surely He will for His glory.

As we go to the houses (especially during the same hours as the church service times), we speak with those who are at home. We don't worry about those who are not home. They may have likely gone to their own churches, so we don't need to reach them with the gospel, especially if they are true followers of Christ.

What to Do When the Weather Interferes

We don't lose the momentum. We pray for people we have already reached and dedicate most of the Sunday service to doing so. Great things are still being accomplished by praying. It's the watering of the seeds we planted as God gives the increase. During such Sundays, emphasize personal evangelism and have people share their experiences. Consider letting people leave early to visit their friends and family to whom they have been ministering and for whom they have been praying. Again, get folks out of the church building to where the people are, to mingle and be the salt. What is being proposed is not new. I call it "the old new way."

In Matthew 9:35-38, Jesus saw the crowd and had compassion on them:

> Then Jesus went about all the cities and villages, teaching in their synagogues, preaching the gospel of the kingdom, and healing every sickness and every disease among the people. But when He saw the multitudes, He was moved with compassion for them, because they were weary and scattered, like sheep having no shepherd. Then He said to His disciples, "The harvest truly is plentiful, but the laborers are few. Therefore, pray the Lord of the harvest to send out laborers into His harvest."

The first thing we note here is how Jesus saw them as "sheep having no shepherd." What does it mean not to have a shepherd? It means that we are clueless and do not know where we are and where we should be going. We know sheep are dumb and need a shepherd to lead and guide. We are clueless about the world we are living in and are trying to navigate without knowing where we are heading. It is just a matter of time before we will crash. We need a shepherd, and His name is Jesus.

Being the Creator, Jesus knows and understands humans more than we understand ourselves. He is not giving His opinion on what human beings need. He speaks of facts. Without knowledge of the Creator, and relating to the Creator and following the Creator, humans are hopeless and most to be pitied. That is exactly why Jesus came and died for us. The Bible also says that Jesus had compassion on the people because they were "weary and scattered." The definition of the word "compassion" is "sympathetic pity and concern for the sufferings or misfortunes of others." Synonyms for "compassion" are the following: pity, sympathy, empathy, fellow feeling, care, concern, solicitude, sensitivity, warmth, love, tenderness, mercy, leniency, kindness, and charity.

Jesus had all of these feelings for the people. We are all weary and scattered. Jesus said, "Come to Me, all you who are weary and burdened, and I will give you rest. Take my yoke upon you and learn from me, for I am gentle and humble in heart, and you will find rest for your souls. For my yoke is easy and my burden is light" (Matthew 11:28-30).

We need Jesus desperately and others need Jesus too. We must have compassion on others who have not yet found rest in Jesus. Without compassion for the lost, we cannot step out of our comfort zone to tell any about Christ. God has not put people in our spheres of influence so that we can see their flaws and criticize them. Rather, God gives us Holy Spirit discernment to see that people really need Him so that we can become intercessors and stand in the gap with prayers and eventually tell them the good news of the gospel.

What to Pray

Notice what Jesus asked the disciples to do: "Therefore, pray the Lord of the harvest to send out laborers into His harvest" (Matthew

9:38). We are not praying to find God's will on whether we should be preaching the gospel; rather, we are asked to pray for release of workers and laborers into the harvest field. God has already made plain His will to seek and save the lost. That's the only reason Jesus came to this world.

Ephesians 2:10 tells us that God has already planned in advance before the ages for us to do this good work. We do not need to hear more sermons about doing the good work of telling someone about Christ; we just need to be obedient and act. We are the answer to Jesus' prayer for workers. We just have to go and obey and tell people of their Savior, Jesus Christ.

Jesus then said, "If you are going to pray this prayer, you, my disciples are the first answer to those prayers." "Calling the Twelve to him, he began to send them out two by two and gave them authority over impure spirits" (Mark 6:7).

As you go, proclaim this message: "The kingdom of heaven has come near. Heal the sick, raise the dead, cleanse those who have leprosy, drive out demons. Freely you have received; freely give" (Matthew 10:7-8).

Later, Jesus went out to preach: "Now it came to pass, when Jesus finished commanding His twelve disciples, that He departed from there to teach and to preach in their cities" (Matthew 11:1). Jesus is never asking us to do what He has not done. Throughout His earthly life, Jesus showed by example how to live and be. He now lives in us and He is doing the same things, if we would yield to His leading and guidance.

The Power to Go

We absolutely need God the Holy Spirit to do and accomplish the "old new" plan proposed here. We cannot do it on our own accord. Jesus told His disciples the same and now reminds us in Acts 1:8: "But you shall receive power when the Holy Spirit has come upon you; and you shall be witnesses to Me in Jerusalem, and in all Judea and Samaria, and to the end of the earth." Likewise, in Luke 24:46, He says, "Behold, I send the promise of My Father upon you; but tarry in the city of Jerusalem until you are endued with power from on high."

It cannot be any clearer than these words. We need to be endued with power from on high. Do we now have the Holy Spirit as promised by Jesus? Yes, we do. The real question is, does the Holy Spirit have us? Are we yielded and surrendered to the Holy Spirit? When He does, the Holy Spirit makes us entirely His so that He delights in us and does whatever He wants through us.

We are not our own. We have been bought at a price (see 1 Corinthians 6:19). We must come to this realization in order for His purposes to be accomplished through us. That's what happened in the book of Acts. First, the disciples obeyed the words of Jesus in Acts 2 and waited as instructed:

When the Day of Pentecost had fully come, they were all with one accord in one place. And suddenly there came a sound from heaven, as of a rushing mighty wind, and it filled the whole house where they were sitting. Then there appeared to them divided tongues, as of fire, and one sat upon each of them. And they were all filled with the Holy Spirit and began to speak with other tongues, as the Spirit gave them utterance.

Peter and the rest realized that they were ordinary fishermen who now had been given over to God by the Holy Spirit. Without God, we can do nothing. And if any person is to be converted and reconciled to God, only God will do it. Otherwise, it will never happen. The disciples became bold and preached with the power of the Holy Spirit and produced God-like results:

- "Then Peter, filled with the Holy Spirit, said to them, 'Rulers of the people and elders of Israel'" (Acts 4:8).
- "And when they had prayed, the place where they were assembled together was shaken; and they were all filled with the Holy Spirit, and they spoke the word of God with boldness" (Acts 4:31).
- "Then Saul, who also is called Paul, filled with the Holy Spirit, looked intently at him" (Acts 13:9).
- "And the disciples were filled with joy and with the Holy Spirit" (Acts 13:52).

The early disciples and converts were able to go from house to house and to wherever the Lord sent them because they were filled with the Holy Spirit and were in "one accord." They also spoke in "our own tongues the wonderful works of God" that carried the message of the gospel. Let's not boast about our being filled with the Holy Spirit or "speaking in tongues" when we can't even speak to our neighbors about Christ and His gospel. Apostle Paul spoke in tongues too and preached the gospel. The purpose for the Holy Spirit being given to us was for us to be living witnesses of Christ and to spread the gospel to the whole world: Parthians, Medes, Elamites, Cretans, Arabs, etc.

We need the same realization and empowerment today as individuals and as the corporate body of Christ to live out the Christian life, to go forth door to door, or in any other form of evangelism the Holy Spirit inspires and leads. Jesus sums it up for us: "I am the vine; you are the branches . . . Remain in Me, and I will remain in you . . . no branch can bear fruit by itself; it must remain in the vine . . . remain in My love . . . I chose you and appointed you to go bear fruit—fruit that will last" (John 15:1-16).

We must keep in mind Jesus' words that precede the "go" in the Great Commission at the end of Matthew: "Jesus came to them and said, 'All authority in heaven and on earth has been given to me. Therefore, go and make disciples.'" The "therefore" implies that we cannot go without being aware of and realizing His power coming from all His authority, both in heaven and on Earth. With the authority of Jesus now present in us in the person of the Holy Spirit, we can go and keep going.

At this point, it's appropriate to ask, have we been doing evangelism on our own strength and power up until now? If we are honest, the answer is yes. We have left the abiding presence of Christ and have been doing our own thing indoors in the church building, producing little or no fruit, and instead experiencing significant decline in church membership. In his article titled "Dispelling the 80 Percent Myth of Declining Churches," Thom S. Rainer, president and CEO of LifeWay Christian Resources, says that 65 percent of churches in America are losing members, are in decline, or have plateaued. That is a significant number. The evidence points to a need for a change that is born out of the indwelling presence of the Spirit of Christ in every believer and follower of Christ.

Lord, we repent and ask You to help us to remain in You that we may bear fruit that will last for eternity—people redeemed by Your blood and whom You have already chosen, just as You chose us.

Under the Influence

We as believers already have the Holy Spirit of Christ. If not, we are not really His. The real issue here is capacity and overflow. We are to be filled and continually be filled with the Holy Spirit. We are to continually yield to the control and leading of the Holy Spirit. Notice in Ephesians 5:17-21 how the apostle Paul compares "drunk with wine" with being "filled with the Spirit." Wine has an intoxicating effect when one is full of it. One who is full of wine is said to be under the "influence" and control of that beverage.

The person is led by the "alcohol spirit." They are not acting and behaving within their normal thinking capacity. Likewise, when we are "filled with the Spirit," our thinking and acting are led and influenced by the Holy Spirit. We must be "intoxicated" and ruled by the Spirit of God who lives in us. When we do, we will overflow with the songs of melody in our hearts, with thanksgiving to our God, and with love by submitting to one another in order to be good witnesses for Jesus.

> *Lord, overflow us this day and in this generation with the Holy Spirit. Lord, take hold of us, for we are Yours. You have bought us at a high price by the blood of Your eternal Son, Jesus Christ.*

We will become rivers of living water as Jesus promised: "He who believes in Me, as the Scripture has said, out of his heart will flow rivers of living water" (John 7:38). Nothing can resist this overflowing river of God coming from Jesus through us. No obstacle, problem or intimidation can resist the overflow of the Spirit of God through us. The gates of Hades shall not prevail against us. Whenever a river encounters an obstacle, it finds another path and even flows with more intensity and broadness. We saw this same thing happen with the disciples in the early church. Because of persecution, they dispersed to various places they would not have gone by their own choosing. When they faced persecution, the church increased even more. For example, in Acts 8:1-8, Philip moved from Jerusalem to Judea and Samaria, after which "multitudes" believed, and signs and wonders followed in healings.

Likewise, in Acts 11:19-21, persecution pushed other disciples from Jerusalem to Phoenicia, Cyprus and Antioch, and there, as they preached, "a great number believed and turned to the Lord."

It is a great place to be under the influence and control of the Holy Spirit. There is no person you cannot speak to when prompted by the Holy Spirit. There is no door you cannot knock on when prompted by the Holy Spirit. And there is no risk you cannot take to share the gospel, knowing that He is in you and with you.

In Matthew 28:20, Jesus exhorts His followers in regard to new believers: "Teaching them to obey everything I have command-ed you. And surely, I am with you always, to the very end of the age." This promise of His presence was given in the context of us "going." As we go to make disciples, Jesus is with us always. Theoretically, we know that Jesus is always with us. I believe we are aware and experience that Jesus is more present with us as we go either door to door or by any other means to proclaim the gos-pel. I can testify to that, as can countless others over the centuries of Christianity. His presence takes away every fear and timidity to proclaim the good news as we go and continue to go and make disciples. With the Holy Spirit present in us, our love for the yet-to-believe/unsaved will overcome the fear of approaching them, for perfect love casts out fear.

The Individual Plan of One-on-One Evangelism

What we do corporately influences what we do as individual Christians. We are first called as a body, the church, the body of Christ. As individual members of the body, we continue what the body does as each member plays his/her part. We get trained to speak to people about Christ when we observe and watch others do it. When we are paired two by two and go out as a corporate body, that is the real school of discipleship. Those who are a little more seasoned are paired with those who are learning.

As we are intoxicated by the influence of the Holy Spirit, we will be full of His joy so that we will spread the gospel where we go: our homes, neighborhoods, communities, schools, workplac-es, ball parks, gyms, and wherever our feet step both physically and electronically. We will be ready at all times, and as Peter said, "[S] anctify the Lord God in your hearts, and always be ready to give a defense to everyone who asks you a reason for the hope that is in you, with meekness and fear" (1 Peter 3:15).

Individual evangelism will flourish among us as we embrace and participate with our brothers and sisters in corporate evangelism. It may take the form of friendship evangelism. It can equally be the on-the-spot sharing of the gospel with strangers we just met or may never meet again, like on a plane. Peter is not necessarily saying to just wait until they ask you before you open your mouth to tell someone of Jesus. The key is being ready at all times and being filled and yielded to the Holy Spirit.

As I write this section, we mourn the home-going of our brother Nabeel Qureshi. As a classmate in medical school, David Wood befriended him and challenged him to investigate the claims of Christ as a historical person and as the Son of God. Nabeel grew up Muslim and by age five could recite the Quran. But God apprehended him in medical school and he found faith in Christ and became a disciple. Nothing is impossible with our God and He can shatter any upbringing and reveal Himself to people using His individual saints and the church collectively. Nabeel died on September 16, 2017, at the age of 34. God used him as a Christian apologist to prosper the gospel, especially among the Muslims.

Imagine the influence of one persistent friend and classmate. You and I can be that person. Someone told you and me. We can tell someone else.

There is a 100 percent guarantee of results for going out and preaching the gospel. You and I are the proof of it. The work is already done by Christ. We are only helping to call people to Christ whom He has already chosen. This is like an exam where we already have the answer sheet. Just fill in the blanks. Will you? Jesus said, "'And I, if I am lifted up from the earth, will draw all peoples to

Myself.' This He said, signifying by what death He would die" (John 12:32-33).

The saving of souls is the easiest thing because it is done by God and not man or woman. The hardest thing is getting up and going to tell the people of the crucified and risen Savior, Jesus. Let's go tell them and let the chips fall where they may. We do not go to "close the deal," so to say. It is a beginning of introduction and invitation to a relationship with God almighty.

The harvest is God's harvest and it is plentiful and ready. As with every harvest, there must be a sense of urgency because the harvest cannot always wait until the next season. No farmer in his right mind would keep postponing his harvest indefinitely or casually pick one ear of corn and then in five years come back for the remaining. No, the farmer deploys all his resources to gather the harvest because it is for an appointed time. Now is the accepted time and today is the day of salvation, not tomorrow.

As individual followers of Christ, let us be ready at all times. Let's carry gospel tracts with us. Let's be friendly to people. Let's find points we have in common with the unsaved and capitalize on those to win their trust. God will use what is in our hands just as He instructed Moses.

Nothing can stop us as we are led by the Holy Spirit. The same words spoken to Zerubbabel are what God speaks to us today: "Not by might, nor by power, but by my Spirit, saith the Lord of hosts" (Zechariah 4:6). The mountain of unbelief in our unsaved loved ones, neighbors and friends can only be broken and come tumbling down by the Spirit of God.

The simple plan is calling us to be true ambassadors of Christ. In the next chapter, let's take a closer look at who an ambassador is and what he/she does.

9

The Ambassadors

M ost countries and kingdoms have ambassadors. Their ambassadors or emissaries are all over the world. The ambassadors represent their nations to the host countries. More specifically, the ambassadors represent the president of their home countries because they are appointed by that president. The ambassadors do not give their personal views on issues, but they speak on behalf of the policies of the president and the nation.

An ambassador is sent. No ambassador exists and fulfills his ambassadorial duties by staying and living in his nation's capital city. The ambassadors must leave and go to the capital city of the nation to which he/she has been appointed and sent. The ambassador has the backing, supplies and empowerment of his/her president to accomplish the mission. We are the ambassadors for Christ. God has sent us to a world that is not our home.

God is doing a new thing and using His church to accomplish His mission in these last days. The resources are available and ready. There was scattered focus in the past but now there will be laser-like focus. The whole body of Christ will be used like never before. The emphasis will come from the pulpits, and the leaders will no longer relegate outreach to the corners and clubs.

We have someone (the Spirit of God) in us who can change people forever. We have something to say to people that can change their lives forever. That is the person of Jesus and we are His ambassadors pleading on His behalf to the world to be reconciled to God. "Now then, we are ambassadors for Christ, as though God were pleading through us: we implore you on Christ's behalf, be reconciled to God" (2 Corinthians 5:20).

Can you imagine the Chinese ambassador to the U.S. walking around Washington, DC, with a gag over his mouth? He walks to the state functions, receives prominent guests and relatives, goes shopping at the local shopping malls and grocery stores, and just lives his life. The only problem is that he is not talking to anyone. In meetings with the State Department and with the American president, he is still gagged. He receives messages from his home country, but he does not relay them. How long do you think such a gagged-mouth ambassador would last as a representative of China?

The Chinese president would have some choices to make. He could tell the ambassador to remove his gag and start speaking, give him time to turn around and do his ambassadorial duties, or just call him back to China. It is possible that some ambassadors of Christ have been called back because they would not speak. It is possible that we as ambassadors of Christ could be called back if we continue to keep silent.

Further imagine that this Chinese ambassador is now talking but he is talking gibberish. Or he speaks but about everything other than the position and wishes of his president. What if he only reflected the American position on issues the Chinese president disagrees with the American president on? Or what if he only talked about the weather, sports, TV shows, sex, money strategies, and the latest fashion in Washington? What if he forgot how to speak Chinese because he rarely speaks to anyone back home or even with other Chinese people in Washington? There would be nothing to show that he was an ambassador and most people would not know him as such. Is it possible this is where most of us are?

Often no one knows us as being ambassadors for Christ. They know us only for other inconsequential and non-lasting things: our professional and job titles, the cars we drive, the neighborhood we live in, our bank accounts. We are not going and living "as though God were pleading through us: we implore you on Christ's behalf, be reconciled to God." Are we "pleading" for God and "imploring" people to turn to God and be reconciled? Pleading and imploring are very active verbs and do not call for silence. God is not on the losing end. The unreconciled is the loser and that is why God in His mercy and love is pleading through us. Someone pleaded with you. Can we return the favor?

The apostle Paul was compelled by Christ's love, and so too must we be. "For the love of Christ compels us, because we judge thus: that if One died for all, then all died; and He died for all, that those who live should live no longer for themselves, but for Him who died for them and rose again" (2 Corinthians 5:14-15).

Jesus clearly defined our primary business and our priority: "But seek first the kingdom of God and His righteousness, and all these things shall be added to you. Therefore, do not worry about tomorrow, for tomorrow will worry about its own things. Sufficient for the day is its own trouble" (Matthew 6:31-34).

We have made "all these things" the priority and have neglected to "seek first the kingdom of God and His righteousness."

Jesus established His kingdom in us and on the Earth. Our priority is to know Him and make Him known. We must advance His kingdom by preaching Christ crucified. It's not Jesus plus something else but the full redemption and justification by the cross of Christ alone.

One of the great advantages of going is the opportunity to first understand and comprehend the gospel for ourselves. If you have not understood it and experienced Christ as your Lord and Savior, then how can you share and explain it to another? Going out will force the unsaved in the pews to be saved, and there are many in that category.

The saved would experience further sanctification as they are forced to reexamine and redefine what they believe. Is it possible that our reluctance to go out in public to declare the gospel message is due to our unwillingness to live out the full gospel? As far as I am a closet Christian, there is no pressure to conform my life to my profession of Christ. The ambassador of any great nation cannot go to another nation to live carelessly, disgracing/embarrassing his king or president.

However, it does not mean that one has to be perfect in order to preach Christ. If this was the criteria, no one would evangelize. The ambassador for Christ is one who has been "reconciled to God" and made a "new creation" by the Holy Spirit. Our being sent is representation of who we are in Christ and it is solely based on this truth: "For He made Him who knew no sin to be sin for us, that we might become the righteousness of God in Him." We reflect the righteousness of Christ as we "go and make disciples."

The Soaking Sponge Experiment

Take four buckets—A, B, C and D—and fill A and B with water. In bucket A, add an orange color. In bucket B, add a green color. Take a big, foamy sponge and immerse it into bucket A. Allow it to soak thoroughly. Remove the sponge from bucket A and squeeze it into bucket C. Soak the sponge a second time in bucket A, but this time don't squeeze it but put it in bucket B to further soak. Take it out from bucket B and squeeze it into bucket D. Compare the color of buckets C and D. You will find that because the sponge was already full of water, the green color in bucket B did not have much effect in changing the color in bucket D.

We are the sponge in bucket D. When you keep taking in and not giving out, you become a "dead sea." The apostle James said not to be just hearers but doers of the Word. We must go out and give what we have freely received. The more we share the gospel, the more we are changed by its power and the more our joy will be full.

Keep Knocking at the Doors

What has been outlined is not a one-month or one-year gospel campaign. This plan is a *continuous* going out. When much ground has been covered and most houses have been visited once, we should start again to revisit the houses we have visited before. We can learn persistency from the Jehovah's Witnesses (JWs) and the Mormons, even though they don't have the truth. They never give up. On average, they knock at our doors at least once a quarter or more.

A friend said to me, "There are some huge questions I have about the door-to-door method. Even the Mormons and JWs are finding it less effective, so I'm curious why you wish to suggest it." Well, the Mormons and the JWs have been doing door-to-door evangelism for a long time. One would expect the world to have been filled with adherents to their false gospel. Thank God that is not the case. Yes, they should know that they have been ineffective not because of their methods but because of their message, which is the false doctrine of God and of who Jesus is.

The JWs and the Mormons do not believe and preach the Christ of the Gospels, who came from heaven, went to the cross, and died to redeem us from sin. The JW's Christ is Michael the archangel or the Christ with a human body who was filled with the spirit of God but is not God. Both JWs and Mormons directly and indirectly deny the deity of Jesus, and that is a falsehood and anti-Christ. The Mormons claim Jesus and Satan are "spirit brothers" born to God the heavenly Father along with a heavenly mother. This is blasphemy and falsehood from the pit of hell. If Jesus Christ is not God, then He would be sinful and an imperfect sacrifice to redeem imperfect humans like us. God required a perfect sinless sacrifice to be a substitute for the sinful human.

As cults, the JWs and Mormons have been ineffective because God is sovereignly guarding His truth and purpose for His creation. The Lord will never allow their false doctrine to prosper and take over the world. It will never save anyone from the wrath of God, and it ties to their good-works basis for salvation.

But we believe Jesus is "The Word became flesh and made his dwelling among us" (John 1:1-3). This is the Jesus we proclaim. As we go door to door and we introduce this Jesus Christ, He confronts and convicts people of their sins and saves them as they put their trust in Him.

A Mormon Encounter

Early on the evening of Saturday, September 23, 2017, two young ladies knocked on our door. I thought it must be Girl Scouts or people doing school fundraising. Behold, they introduced themselves as Mormon missionaries. I greeted and welcomed them and sat on the steps while they gave me their Mormon gospel. They said Jesus was the Son of God and He died for all of us so that we can have better lives and families, that God gave prophets, that Jesus was a good prophet like Moses, and that God gave another prophet, Joseph Smith, who came to set the church straight. I allowed them to speak for a while and listened carefully without interrupting. That is how I earned my right to speak.

I asked if they believed every word of the Bible, and they said yes. Did they believe that Jesus is God? They said that Jesus is a god and that they believe in the Father, the Son and the Holy Ghost. So, I asked that if Jesus is a god but not the God, then is it true we have many gods? I asked if they had read the Bible, especially Revelation 22 where it says not to add to Scripture; so why would they consider the Book of Mormon as Scripture? They claimed that an angel gave Joseph Smith the revelation. Okay, but an "angel" also gave Muhammad, the founder of Islam, a revelation as well. Back to Joseph Smith: I asked why they would follow someone who would not even obey the Bible and married so many wives. I asked the two of them if they would be happy to be second, third or fourth wives. They said no but that God commanded Joseph Smith to marry many wives but that they do not practice that right now. They saw that they were going nowhere and not making sense and they concluded, as they usually do, that they had their beliefs and I have my beliefs and we should both pray to find the truth. I pitied the young women and said to them to please seek objective truth and stick with the Bible. By now, they were in a hurry to leave. They were out of our cul-de-sac in a second.

Seeing the zeal of these young ladies to propagate lies and falsehood, I am more determined than ever to knock on doors and preach the true gospel. What excuses do we have not to go and preach it? If we are the true church, then we must go and make disciples and knock on every door. We cannot stay silent while the Mormons and the Jehovah's Witnesses go around to confuse our neighbors with lies from the pit of hell while we sit with truth in our church buildings and homes. The Mormons gave me a booklet titled *The Restoration of the Gospel of Jesus Christ*. It is full of lies and misuse of Scripture. This booklet says:

[The book of Mormon is] a record of God's dealings with the ancient inhabitants of the Americas and contains, as does the Bible, the fullness of the everlasting Gospel ... The Book of Mormon is a powerful witness of Jesus Christ. It helps understand His teachings, including those in the Bible.

This is the garbage that is being fed to our neighbors.

Lord, help us to offer Your truth to people.

My JW Encounter

One Saturday morning, two ladies in their late forties or early fifties showed up. One was obviously more seasoned than the other. I opened the door and they asked me, "Do you like all the troubles going on in the world right now? Would you not like something better where there is peace and no troubles?"

I said, "Sure, I would like peace." They proceeded to tell me how and flashed their pamphlet to me. We were still outside on the door steps, so I said, "Please come in and have a seat to explain it to me." They were surprised that I invited them inside. I like to be nice to them because I would expect people to be nice to me as we go door to door with the real truth.

While seated, they proceeded to show me in their Bible where peace is promised and where there will be no more troubles. I told them to wait so that I could follow with my own Bible, so I grabbed mine. They read from Revelation 21:4: "And God will wipe away every tear from their eyes; there shall be no more death, nor sorrow, nor crying. There shall be no more pain, for the former things have passed away." The rookie was leading and said, "Wouldn't you love that?" I said, "Yes, I would love to have no more pain and tears. Can we read from the beginning of the chapter so that we can see who the promise is for and to put it all in context?"

I read from Revelation 21:1-3, where it says that the promise is for the bride of Christ, "His people," I said. "Are you a bride of Christ?" They said no. The more experienced JW said that the bride is a special group and that they are not part of the bride of Christ.

"If you are not the bride of Christ, and this promise does not apply to you, then why are you going around promising people a better tomorrow?" I asked.

I asked if they believed and trusted Jesus Christ as Lord and Savior. They said they believe Jesus is the Savior and died for all.

"Do you believe that the same Jesus Christ is God?" I asked. They said He is not because God cannot die.

"Then, who is this Jesus?" I asked. They responded that He is the Son of God.

"Isn't He an angel as you believe?" I asked. The JWs clearly teach and believe that Jesus is created and not the Creator. They quote Colossians 1:15, "firstborn over all creation," and refuse to acknowledge the truth in verse 18, "firstborn from the dead," referring to Jesus' resurrection. For them, Jesus is Michael the archangel.

The ladies became very uncomfortable and said that they had not come to do in-depth Bible study with me or others in the neighborhood; but if I wanted, I should come to their kingdom hall to learn more. They got up to leave and I asked them to not come back until they had found and accepted the true Jesus Christ, who is not an angel. The two ladies hurried out and left.

We truth bearers can no longer allow the JWs or the Mormons to peddle this nonsense to our neighbors. I can imagine an unsuspecting neighbor accepting their garbage of lies. We must go door to door so that people will know the true Jesus and that the JWs and Mormons do not have the truth. We must confront the JWs and Mormons with the truth and not run from them. Paul said to contend for the faith, and we must.

As we keep on going back to knock on the same doors, we will more likely find someone at home who was not there the first or second time. When we go back and knock and run into the same people—even if with a different team of two from church—people will know that we are serious and that our message is too important to leave them alone. It may seem annoying but let's annoy people into heaven and give them a chance to meet Jesus Christ, who alone can transform their lives. We should saturate our locality with the gospel so that no one will have an excuse.

It is important to keep in mind that it takes multiple encounters for many to give serious thought and consideration to the message of the gospel. We live in an electronic age where many things are capturing the attention of people, including the very young. There is so much entertainment to distract one's attention and most (unfortunately, including people in the church) are preoccupied with their electronic gadgets. You as a believer can look back and see how many encounters it took before Christ got your attention.

For me, it was many approaches and many knockings on the door of my heart before I was awakened to the truth of Christ. We should not expect anything different from those who are yet to come to faith and trust in God. The farmer does not quit planting because some seeds did not come forth from the ground in one year or even if there is a crop failure in one year. The farmer keeps on tilling the ground, planting, watering, weeding, and harvesting year after year. So we must never give up but continuously go and keep going and making disciples for Christ.

Imagine Joshua and the Israelites giving up after the first march around Jericho before the wall fell. "And the LORD said to Joshua: 'See! I have given Jericho into your hand, its king, and the mighty men of valor. You shall march around the city, all you men of war; you shall go all around the city once. This you shall do six days'" (Joshua 6:2-3).

Our Father God has already given His Son, Jesus Christ, "the nations for His inheritance" and "the ends of the earth for His possession" (Psalm 2). We are calling people whom God has already chosen and has already called to Jesus. God had already given Jericho to the people of Israel. We are knocking and marching around to break down the walls of blindness, hardness of heart, and unbelief. The walls are surely coming down by the power of the Holy Spirit. Please don't stop marching and knocking.

We have outlined the plan for the corporate church and for individuals. The corporate plan is a simple one to use at least one Sunday every month to spread the gospel, evangelizing door to door. Through that, individuals will be equipped to do the one-on-one evangelism wherever they may be. In addition, individuals may be inspired to go into foreign missions to reach the "unreached" peoples of this world. We cannot go on our own. We must be empowered and intoxicated by the Holy Spirit in order to go and keep going. Going door to door at least one Sunday a month will require some preparations by the local congregation before it can be embraced and implemented.

10

Preparations

I am reminded of where it says in Psalm 127, "Unless the LORD builds the house, they labor in vain who build it; Unless the LORD guards the city, the watchman stays awake in vain." If the Lord does not capture the hearts of His people, then the change we desire and expect will not happen. Only the Holy Spirit can convict and convince God's people to embrace the simple plan. Otherwise, there will be a strong push-back by those who love the status quo.

There should be discussions among the church leadership in board meetings and any available forums to pray about and discuss this major paradigm shift. There will always be those on the fence who are struggling with the concept, but for the sake of Christ, they will give it a chance.

One of the keys to the success of this simple plan is to prepare and present the concept from the pulpit. The gospel mission is our core business and we are not ashamed of it. First, the concept has to be introduced to the congregation weeks in advance of the first outing. Where there are multiple pastors, we recommend that the senior pastor introduce the idea of going out at least one Sunday every month. At least two other subsequent weeks can be used to teach and rehearse from the pulpit with skits and question-and-answer sessions.

Leaders must have repentant hearts in explaining this whole idea of being and doing church differently. We must own up to our sins in participating and aiding in incestuous Christianity. I know that most of what we currently do in church and how we do it was passed down to us. We should still apologize to the congregation, ask for forgiveness, and together pray for the grace to move forward in making disciples as Jesus commanded. We must go in the strength of humility that comes from Christ and as He demonstrated for us. Let's be encouraged by the words of apostle Paul:

> Let this mind be in you which was also in Christ Jesus, who, being in the form of God, did not consider it robbery to be equal with God, but made Himself of no reputation, taking the form of a bondservant, and coming in the likeness of men. (Philippians 2:5-11)

The Gospel Message and Presentation

The gospel message must be explained in the clearest and simplest terms that even our teenagers can use. If we can't understand it, then we cannot explain it to people on the streets. The apostle Paul summarized the gospel message in 1 Corinthians 15:1-9.

We must establish immediately why anyone needs Jesus. If there is no need for Jesus, then there is no need for preaching the gospel. If I do not understand my sinful nature and alienation from God and consequent separation from the Father, then I will not understand why I need a Savior. Jesus came to seek and save the lost and reconcile them back to a holy God who cannot tolerate any lack of holiness or sin. We need Jesus because we all have sinned, and none is righteous.

How do we present this gospel to this generation that has no concept of the word "sin" in their daily living and cultural vocabulary? Rabbi Eric H. Yoffie, president emeritus of the Union of Reformed Judaism, wrote in the *Huffington Post* an article titled "Why Americans Dismiss Sin." He observed, "The United States is a religious country, and one might think that sin would be a major subject of public discourse. Yet this is not so. We may talk of 'morality,' but being moral is generally a secular matter, cleansed of any hint of evil or sinfulness. And, oddly enough, even in religious circles, we fear the language of sin and rush to avoid it." I would add that the West and most parts of the world hardly use the word "sin" in public media forums. To say to someone that "all have sinned" may not mean anything to the person.

The Reverend Jonathan Dodson of City Life Church in Austin, Texas, suggests learning new language and biblical metaphors that make the gospel believable and relevant to this generation. As he says in his article published on the Desiring God website titled "Evangelism on the Rocks, "To those seeking tolerance, the atonement offers a redemptive tolerance that gives progressive people an opportunity to experience grace and forgiveness in a way that doesn't demean other faiths, which can be very liberating."

I am also a firm believer that the Holy Spirit who resides in us gives us words to speak to specific people whom we encounter in our outreach efforts. After all, it is not our message, and if we listen to the Sender, then we will hear, deliver and speak as prompted.

As part of the preparation, the gospel message should be presented to the congregation from the pulpit if it isn't already being regularly done. Let those who have not trusted in Christ put their faith in the living Savior. For those who are already followers of Christ, let it be a reaffirmation and solidification of their understanding of the gospel message.

Skits and Rehearsals

Jonathan Dodson, previously cited, said "the gospel is slowly associated with forceful Christians who are information-driven, looking to get Jesus off their chest." It is more obligation than passion. To the unbelieving, there is no perfectly polite way of sharing the gospel with them. However, we Christians are people filled with the Holy Spirit of self-control, discernment, love and respect.

We must do our best not to be robotic in our approach and interactions with people. We are not on a class assignment to earn points for every encounter. We must understand the basic gospel message, what it means to us, and how we have experienced Christ as a witness.

Our experience going door to door has been very rewarding and joyful. Our approach has been of respect to the homeowners. When they are willing to talk or even a little reluctant to talk, we ask questions and do less talking ourselves. It is a dialogue and not a deluge of information transfer. Jesus employed open-ended questions as He interacted with people. In interacting with the woman at the well (see John 4), it was more of a dialogue with questions and answers. The woman told Jesus who she was by responding to His questions.

When we ask questions and listen to the people's answers, they feel heard. Their answers lead us to the next question or comment. We are trying to understand the people's faith journey or faithless journey.

Let's now look at some skits of scenarios we may encounter. There may be skits on when the door is slammed on us and the people say, "I don't want to talk to you." How does one respond in such a scenario? At the very least, we can smile. Another skit may be at a home where the resident says, "We are already going to church, but we cannot talk right now." Again, we should smile, thank them and, if possible, offer a tract or flyer to them.

A third skit could be an inquiring household open to listening or at least to sharing in prayer. In this case the skit can expand the interaction by asking open-ended questions. Where people accept an offer to be prayed for, it is best to pray first and then follow up with questions that can lead to more discussion. Whenever we hear the response, "I am trying my best to please God," that is an open indication to pursue further interaction.

A fourth skit would be when we are invited to come in but the resident is only interested in arguments. We are not there to argue but to proclaim. We should make every effort to understand where the people are coming from and what they have to say. When the people are contentious, we can quickly excuse ourselves and leave.

Create room for dialogue during the Sundays used for preparation. The church members may ask any questions or state objections about going out to preach in homes door to door. We should never be afraid of the questions. Let someone record the questions and if there are no immediate answers, let one be brought back the next Sunday. Most people have never gone door to door to proclaim the gospel, so we must allow sufficient time for people to ask questions to calm their fears. No one should ever feel that this idea is being forced on them. We must allow the Holy Spirit to do His work of teaching and bringing understanding to any believer. Let's trust the Father, who said to pray for workers/harvesters to send into the ready harvest field. God will send His people.

No-Solicitation Signs, Gated Communities and Apartment Complexes

At this point, let's address the issue of dealing with no-solicitation signs, gated communities, and apartment complexes. Use your judgment and wisdom as the Holy Spirit prompts. People have handled it in various ways. A question posted on baptistboard. com was: "Is door-to-door evangelism soliciting?" Many said yes; many said no. One of the respondents said, "The legal definition of soliciting requires that you are 'soliciting' for something tangible . . . money, donations, etc. It does not include evangelism." I like this answer and I have knocked at doors with no-solicitation signs. Sometimes no one answers the door; other times someone does. I remember one incident where we had a very meaningful and respectful conversation with the resident.

It's a bit more complicated with regards to gated communities and apartment complexes. You have to be let into these places. We should pray and seek favor with the property managers to ask permission to knock on doors. In addition, other methods of outreach should be considered for those places. God loves people living in gated communities and apartments. Maybe the believers living in such places can focus on reaching their community or apartment. Our lives and where we live are no coincidence, for the steps of the righteous are ordered by God.

Materials to Share

In advance, decide on the literature and hand-outs to be used. Design or order some very good gospel tracts. Back in the 1970s, for example, Jews for Jesus designed their own tracts, called "broadsides," to be handed out on the street. Instead of looking mass-produced, these were materials that named the city where the people lived and spotlighted a local situation that everyone could identify with. They were quite clever. Consideration should be given to materials that can be hung on the door knob if residents are not home when we knock. Try your materials out, as there are a variety of knobs out there.

Whatever material is handed out should have identification: the name of the church, its address, its phone number, and its website address. One can order a simple rubber stamp with relevant information that is used to stamp all tracts and materials being handed out.

By investing in tracts or other literature for outreach, we are putting our money where our mouth is. There will be initial and ongoing costs for implementation. Since the gospel is our priority and primary business, it deserves the necessary resources.

The literature and materials should be passed around so that members are familiar with it and can read the materials before going out. People will ask about the content when you try to give out materials.

Going Two by Two

The pairing of two by two is also a form of discipleship. The goal is to pair people with experience with those who have never done door-to-door evangelism before. Being that most people in the church may not have gone door to door before, it may not be possible to always have an experienced person along. Married couples can be paired together. Where spouses are not available, and/or the people are single saints, we suggest men be paired with men and women be paired with women. If possible, pair people up ahead of the going-out day so that less time is used for that purpose on the outreach day. If someone does not show up, then that can be dealt with on the day of the outreach. We suggest that pairs exchange phone/text numbers to communicate and also pray together before the day of the outreach.

There may from time to time arise issues of tensions between the evangelizing pairs. There may be disagreements. Even if you disagree with your partner on something that comes up in a conversation with the person being visited, do *not* show any tension or anything other than unity. Discuss your disagreements later.

Obtain neighborhood maps where they are available. With smartphones, we have most maps at our fingertips. Some of the apps have the individual houses on every street. If possible, print maps of the streets that are assigned to various teams for a database of encounters, results, and names of people to pray for in each house. Familiarize the congregation with the neighborhood.

Let's be culturally sensitive. Although there are differences between yours and other cultures, we still owe all people the gospel. If they open their doors, we cannot just walk away because they are different or may be of a different religion. We still say why we came, and if they insist on not talking with us, we thank them. At least ask how we can pray for them before leaving that house or person. An example of being culturally sensitive is to know that most Muslim women (especially from the Middle East) would not extend their hands to shake the hand of a man they do not know. I found out the hard way after being embarrassed during outreach. Orthodox Jewish men, should you encounter any, will not shake the hand of a woman who is not their wife.

Even transportation logistics must be thought about ahead of time. This becomes more critical the farther we go from the church building to the neighborhoods. The ideal would be for everyone to drive to wherever we are going. But that is not wise and practical. We must be mindful of congesting the neighborhood with so many cars that it becomes a problem for residents to freely get around. Where the streets visited are very close to the church, we should walk to these homes.

The next consideration would be pooling people together into bigger cars and vans to get where we are going. The last option should be using a church bus or any bus to drop people off at a designated point and then come back to pick them up when the outreach is over. I know that God has various gifted people in the area of logistics who would come up with better plans of getting people safely to destinations and back. The main point here is to think and plan for transportation ahead of time.

Pray and Pray

Praying is key. Praying is also the actual work. It would be very naïve and foolish to think that the shift from incestuous Christianity to making disciples would take place without consistent praying. The first prayer is for our repentance and turning around to do what God designed for us to do from the foundation of the world.

We must pray for our pastors, church leaders, and all of God's people to catch the vision of what God is doing during these end times. The scripture says that without a vision, the people perish. Vision comes when we look to God through the eyes of prayer and His Word, such as Jeremiah 33:3, which says, "Call to Me, and I will answer you, and show you great and mighty things, which you do not know."

We are not selling a product here. The gospel is not a project, either. We are trying to reach people, all of whom belong to God. Jesus is their Savior and we are not. He will call them to Himself, so let's call them to Christ in prayers before we step out to meet them in person.

Several days before going to a certain neighborhood, a couple of people should drive through the streets praying for the people and houses for open hearts and doors. Pray for welcoming favors. Pray for God to disarm all principalities and powers in operation in the neighborhood. Pray blessings on the people for healings of marriages and hurts and for the children.

This is warfare and advance surveillance-mission prayer before the "assault." These prayers point to where our strength lies and comes from. We must therefore be fully armed with the whole armor of God. Ephesians 6:10-20, which describes this, ends with a prayer that "I may open my mouth boldly to make known the mystery of the Gospel."

We must realize who the enemy is. The unbelieving and wayward are not the enemy, whether they are in our families or on the streets. Many of us used to be the unbelieving and wayward. Let's not ever forget where we came from. The real enemy is Satan and his cohorts. "For we do not wrestle against flesh and blood, but against principalities, against powers, against the rulers of the darkness of this age, against spiritual hosts of wickedness in the heavenly places." It is Satan who has blinded the eyes of the unbelieving from seeing God. We pray and God fights them for us and removes the spiritual blindness so that those we go to receive the gospel. Satan and his cohorts are already defeated on the cross, so our victory is sure and already secured. We are marching along with and following the victor, Jesus Christ.

Like Paul, we must ask for and pray that utterance and boldness be given to us to speak the gospel. We pray that people will understand us and hear what the Spirit is saying to them, regardless of style or presentation.

Continuous Prayer

The prayers do not stop after the outreach. We continue to pray for the people and the community after each outreach. We pray for the names we gathered during the outreach and we continue to pray for the specifically expressed prayer request of the people with whom we talked.

I don't pretend to have covered everything there is in preparation for implementation. We must trust the Father who has called us to this work, His harvest. We must pray and continue to pray for all things and everything and at all times without ceasing.

Will God answer? You bet He will. The Lord has guaranteed to hear us and answer every prayer that is according to His will. The promise is for those who believe and trust in Jesus as the Messiah, the Christ. Have we trusted and believed Jesus? Yes. The apostle John writes to assure us that we belong to God and that, as His children, He hears and answers us (see 1 John 5:13-15).

What things do we know for sure are according to God's will? When Jesus instructs you to pray for something, that is definitely God the Father's will. In the context of this whole book and the paradigm shift called for, we are guaranteed success because it is in accordance with God's will. How do I know? Hear Jesus again: "The harvest is plentiful but the workers are few. Ask the Lord of the harvest, therefore, to send out workers into his harvest field" (Matthew 9:37-38).

Let's believe and watch God do it. I am not dreaming. I have confidence in the Father of the harvest. We must believe Jesus and trust Him. Let us continue to obey the injunction of the apostle Paul not to be anxious but to pray with thanksgiving to God (see Philippians 4:6-7). Sharing the gospel can bring anxiety, so we must pray for the boldness and peace that come from God to do His work. Don't be anxious; just pray and thank God for the people He has brought into your path, and surely He will answer us.

We will not remain in the church building to party with the 99 but instead will go with Jesus to look for the one who is lost, and we will pray for them.

Christ loves all and cares for all, so we must love all and care for all. Everyone is very important to God, whether they are a Democrat, a Republican, a reprobate, an Independent, black, white, brown, yellow, rich or poor. God only sees two classes of people: the saved and the lost. Let's go beyond the labels and love people and tell them the gospel. It does not matter what label we have; if we don't have Christ and are not saved, then we are headed to hell.

We must pray for all people. "I urge, then, first of all, that petitions, prayers, intercession and thanksgiving be made for all people—for kings and all those in authority, that we may live peaceful and quiet lives in all godliness and holiness. This is good, and pleases God our Savior, who wants all people to be saved and to come to a knowledge of the truth" (1 Timothy 2:1-4).

Lord, we pray for all today. Help us to continue to pray for the leaders of nations and for all people that they will come to the knowledge of the truth. Save people by revealing Yourself to them by the power of Your Holy Spirit. Amen.

11

Does It Work?

When I got the idea of going door to door to preach the gospel in America and of involving the *entire* church instead of a few evangelism club members, I was excited; but deep within, I had some fears. I had spoken to people individually during street evangelism and other outreach efforts. However, I had never gone knocking door to door to tell anyone about the love of Jesus in America.

My door-to-door evangelism experience goes way back to when I first trusted Jesus as my Savior and went door to door with some seasoned Christians to preach in Nigeria, my country of birth. That was more than 37 years ago. First, it is very necessary at this point to tell you about the transforming power of the gospel in my own life before I show evidence of the gospel in others' lives.

I was born in a loving family where we were brought up in the church. My mother and father attended the African Methodist Episcopal Zion Church. My siblings and I went with my uncle to the Catholic church because it had formal education and schooling for children. My earliest memories are of going with my parents to their church until I was of school age, first grade. In our village, going to church was a social thing and the day we got to wear our church clothes and shoes that we never wore during the week.

Growing up in the Catholic church and schooling, we were taught catechism and good behaviors. We went to church every Sunday. Our primary school teachers and the church catechist were responsible for teaching us about God and things of religion. Maybe once a quarter, the priest would come to our particular village to say Mass for us. The adults would receive Holy Communion during those services, which I longed to do as well. I eventually did after being baptized and then confirmed at around 11 years old. I loved going to church to meet friends and play after church.

I played the "church game" as a teenager and then went to a boarding high school that was far from my village. It was my first time living in a house with electricity and regular plumbing. At the end of each semester, I would return to our home in the village. I looked forward to seeing family and old friends. During these times, two of my cousins who had become born again would speak to me about Jesus and would ask me to put my faith in Him. I never understood what they were saying because I never listened or gave them a chance. We would laugh at them and make fun of them. We called them names and said, "Oh now you are following 'those people' who are always carrying their Bibles." The Bible was not a book I read nor was I really exposed to one. All of my religious knowledge at that time was passed down through the church.

On one of those holiday breaks from high school, my cousin told me about a gospel crusade in a nearby village that was organized by the Scripture Union. My cousin told me that there was going to be a movie. That got my attention, for I was a teenager who did not have much going for entertainment during vacation. I was sold and committed to going to the crusade. Keep in mind, we did not have other forms of entertainment such as television, since there was no electricity in the village at that time.

The Jesus film they showed us captured my attention. Afterward, the preacher explained the gospel to the crowd. For the first time, I heard the truth of the gospel loud and clear. I understood for the first time that my good works were never sufficient to please God or for Him to let me off the hook for the penalties of my sin. Also, if I died that night, I would go to hell if I did not place my trust and faith in Jesus who died for my sins. The Jesus film had already dramatized the death and suffering of Jesus for me. I had no struggle at the end of that night to place my trust in Jesus. The preacher called out for those who had made a commitment and I went forward with many others. My new relationship with my God, my creator and lover Jesus Christ, began on December 26, 1976. I thank God that since then, I have never regretted being found by Jesus. I don't want to say I found Jesus and I only said yes to His invitation. He chose me for a new life and an eternal life with Him before the world began. I am forever grateful, owe Him my life, and am committed to helping Him call others of His children whom He already has chosen.

I am forever grateful to my cousins, to Scripture Union, and to the believers who helped disciple us new believers. I acquired a Bible and hungered to read and study it. They taught us the Bible and introduced us to evangelism and how to tell all our friends what had happened to us and our new relationship with Jesus. The seasoned Christians took us on door-to-door evangelism to our villages to tell others about the good news of Christ. Being a new believer, initially I was afraid, but the more we went out, the more

I gained confidence. Also, it was a declaration to my friends, relatives, and the "unseen forces" that I now belonged to Christ and to a new family of the body of Christ. I had become one of "those people" who carried their Bibles around and was not ashamed to be seen carrying the Bible. I had now joined the laughing stock of the village and would be called the names I used to call my cousins and people like them.

After being in America for more than 37 years, I still had not been door to door. The thought terrified me, though I have done it before in Nigeria. What had America done to my faith in 37 years with regards to evangelism? Only the Jehovah's Witnesses knocked on doors in America. I supposed they had a patent on door-to-door evangelism in America and the rest of the West.

A lot of my fears were inflicted by people I shared the idea of door-to-door evangelism with, as they themselves were scared by the thought. Things like, "There are crazy people out there in America who may have guns who could shoot if you disturbed them. Oh, they will never open their doors; people are too particular about their privacy and will not welcome you." There are a thousand-and-one reasons not to go knocking on people's doors. I am writing to report that God conquered all my fears by just trying it and doing it.

Small/Home-Group Fellowship Outreach Efforts

Forcey Bible Church, our home church in Silver Spring, Maryland, has home groups. My wife and I lead one of them. When I started writing this book, I shared with the home group what was on my heart and they encouraged me and we prayed. I told them that with their permission I would like to start putting into practice the idea of door-to-door evangelism. Why write and talk about door-to-door outreach if I am not willing to test it and try it? We did and it works all the time by the power of the Holy Spirit.

We started going door to door on Sunday afternoons close to the same time we would ordinarily meet for home-group fellowship. The idea is not to duplicate and multiply meeting sessions, since everyone is already busy. The door-to-door outreach would be in place of a regularly scheduled meeting. Prior to the first outing, we did some refreshing on what the gospel is all about and rehearsed various possible scenarios of encounters at the homes of people in the neighborhood.

We discussed which streets to start with and why. I proposed that we start with our "Jerusalem," meaning we would start with each member's street and then after that we would go to other streets in the neighborhood. Of course, we had to start with my street, since it was my idea. I felt terrified. What would my neighbors say? Would they now see me as a religious fanatic?

I had been doing the surveillance praying as preparation. For years, I have been praying for God to apprehend my neighbors and reveal Himself to them. Now the rubber would meet the road as we would be going door to door on my street. We paired up, got our materials, prayed, and started knocking on doors. I was paired up with a brother who did not live on our street. My wife, UD, was paired up with another sister. My nine-year-old daughter, Grace, joined us. (We should pass on this passion for preaching and making disciples to our children as early as possible.)

My fears never went away until we knocked on the first door. No one was home at the first house. Silently, I thanked God, as I had dodged the first bullet. We left a tract at the door. At the second house, our neighbor was home. I introduced us, since the neighbor knew me. I had been praying for this neighbor and had had conversations with him about putting his faith in Christ. This time, I let my brother in Christ who was paired up with me speak to him. My neighbor, who I will call EJ, said that he had been exploring some Universalist churches. He was not convinced that Christ was the only option. He said that he had been raised as a Catholic and that he had lost faith and hope in that church because of things he and others had been through in the Catholic Church. He quickly told us about his disappointment with organized religion. He said he was more interested in spirituality, which we agreed was different from religion. When we asked how he would arrive at an answer, he said it would be by trying and exploring options. We encouraged him to keep seeking but to seek to find who Jesus is for him and not what others tell him. We thanked him for speaking with us.

By now, my fears had vanished, and I felt some boldness. We went to the next house and the door was opened. We had a great conversation and found out that this neighbor and family had real faith in Christ and used to go to the church we now attend. Their kids were raised in the church. They now go to another church, but I don't think their adult children are following along. We usually ask if there are things to pray for the family, so we were requested to pray for sick family members. We prayed right on the spot.

Eventually, we returned to our house and recounted our stories and prayed for all to whom we had spoken and for the homes where we had left gospel tracts where the people were not home. I was not the only one who had had fears before going out. At the end of the first outing, all our fears were gone just because we stepped out in faith ready to suffer shame and ridicule for Christ. We were all surprised that the people were nice to us and welcomed us, and we prayed with some of the families. We all agreed to do it again.

We have now gone several times door to door on different Sundays. We are currently following a bi-weekly schedule during the spring, summer and fall. There have only been a few instances when people have refused to open the door or have decided not to talk with us. For those who do talk to us, it is a conversation and not really a telling. We ask the people open-ended questions and allow them to tell their own stories. We follow up with more questions to engage them to think through what they are saying. Nothing is now stopping us and we all look forward to going out to share the gospel door to door.

We have met all kinds of people and have heard all kinds of faith journeys and experiences. We have conversed with Hindus, Buddhists, Muslims, agnostics, Christians, cultural Christians, the "nones" (those who do not identify with any religion and who are a growing population in the West), and more.

On our second outreach, we met an agnostic (Mr. R), who was a young man in his early thirties. He did not grow up in a religious home. He told us that he knew that there was a higher being but that he does not know who He is. He added that he was not searching but that he was open at some point in the future. We thanked him for being candid with us and left his house. One home-group member sees Mr. R from time to time since they live on the same street. We all continue to pray for him and all whom we have encountered this way.

God, by the power of His Holy Spirit, has transformed us ordinary church members and former pew-warmers and spectators into witnesses for Christ. We no longer dread going out to tell our neighbors about the gospel. There is great joy among us and in us. We rejoice, keeping in mind what Jesus said to His disciples after a successful outreach: "Nevertheless, do not rejoice in this, that the spirits are subject to you, but rather rejoice because your names are written in heaven" (Luke 10:20).

We were made aware of some kids' needs for back-to-school supplies while going door to door. By God's sovereign provisions, we met those needs in follow-up visits. There was a lady who thought we were angels. She had been alone and worried and thinking about her grandson who was in the hospital. She believed in Christ but was not attending any church. She was overjoyed to see us and welcomed us into her home. She said that she knew God sent us to encourage her. We prayed with her for her grandson, who had a brain aneurysm. A week later, we followed up to check how her grandson was doing. He was being released from the hospital the same day and was doing much better. We rejoiced together and thanked God.

Has anyone prayed the sinner's prayer? Not yet, but we are reaching people, most of whom do not attend church and have not been confronted with the gospel. We have prayed with many for their various needs and have trusted God to answer. As I already mentioned, we are not going necessarily to close the deal. We have spoken to many and given them gospel tracts. We are praying and committing them to God, who knows them very well and who will do the work of conviction and saving and drawing them to Himself. It is an exciting day to be speaking to people about Christ when many voices are silent about Christ.

Since we have gone door to door several times now, we are learning along the way. We usually introduce ourselves and ask for the names of people we meet. Most give us their first names. We already know their addresses, so we are now following up with handwritten thank-you notes. We tailor the notes to the conversations we had and express our thanks for their willingness to speak with us.

Congregational Gospel Outreach Efforts

There are churches that are having great success in door-to-door evangelism. Under the heading "Mythbuster: Louisville pastor triples attendance in 6 months by knocking on doors," we read some great news. Here is an excerpt of what was reported by Robin Cornetet in *Kentucky Today:*

> A Louisville pastor has busted the longstanding myth in the church world that door-to-door visitation is out of vogue and no longer effective.

Mark Bishop has knocked on about 200 doors a week since he arrived six months ago at Highview Baptist Church—Valley Station Campus. In that time, he has baptized 37 new believers and has seen attendance triple to nearly 300 people.

"In this electronic age, people are shocked that I would take the time to stop by their house to talk to them in person," said Bishop, a strong advocate for so-called front porch evangelism . . .

With the help of members spending their Sunday evenings going door-to-door, Bishop said the church has stood on more than 5,000 welcome mats—even in the rare instance when they weren't all that welcome.

"I think soul winning is easier caught than taught," Bishop said, referring to the newfound evangelical fervor at the church. "When they see it working, it becomes contagious."

This is awesome. I had the joy of speaking with pastor Mark Bishop. Mark is so excited and willing to multiply this success all over the world. He is willing to visit any church to help coach them on how to get going.

In the same article, Robin Cornetet also reported about a broader effort by the state Baptist Convention in deploying conference attendees to evangelism:

"There is nothing better than one-on-one contact when sharing Jesus," said Kentucky Baptist Convention Executive Director Paul Chitwood. "While I am a firm believer in mass evangelism and pulpit evangelism, both will almost always involve one-on-one evangelism." Chitwood said plans are underway for a similar evangelistic outreach held in conjunction with this year's Kentucky Baptist Convention annual meeting in Louisville. Crossover Louisville will involve a massive door-to-door campaign with members of KBC churches across the state coming into city days in advance of the Nov. 14 meeting to share the Gospel . . . "Every Christian isn't called to preach to the masses," Chitwood said, "but every Christian is called to share Jesus at every opportunity."

Workplace Bible Study Group

By the special grace of God, I have led a Bible study group at work for more than 23 years. We dedicated the first Thursday of the month for gospel outreach instead of gathering for Bible study. I wanted us to walk the walk of what I have written—that is, that we use any major gatherings for Bible study or conferences to reach people for Christ.

Since we are at a workplace (and lunch time is very limited), we are asking members to be intentional on this day to identify and have lunch with someone who is not a believer and a follower of Christ. We are to use the time to cultivate friendship with the intent of sharing the gospel. The following week, we report and share testimonies of what happened. We then pray for the names of people encountered the previous week.

We have done this for several months now and there are testimonies to share in this section. Because of my June 2016 stroke, I had been working from home in our tele-work program. However, this did not stop me from participating and leading the group. I have gone on my own on these gospel outreach Thursdays to visit my elderly neighbors who are home during lunch time. I have also chosen to go to the shopping center near our house at different times. I have used that time to pass out gospel tracts and speak to anyone who is willing to stop for a minute or two to listen.

On one occasion, I gave out tracts to many until I encountered "Roy," a young man in his late twenties/early thirties. I gave him a tract that asked, "Where will you spend eternity?" He gave me a disdainful look and kept walking into a store, telling me no. I continued approaching and giving tracts to others and having some interesting quick conversations with the people who were moving very fast either due to being on a brief lunch break or whatever. I had a very probing quick discussion with a Jewish lady who said she cannot believe because she is Jewish. I reminded her that Jesus was Jewish and likewise all the disciples. She asked about a Second Coming, so I told her that if she is waiting (to accept Christ) until then, it will be too late for her. She said that that is what we (Christians) believe, that she does not believe this, and she entered her car. I thanked her for speaking with me.

Well, back to Roy. He came out of the store and I approached him again and said, "My friend, I still have good news for you." He said he was not interested and that I was invading his space. He went on to say that he knows God too and that what I was doing was not the way to lead others to Him. I asked him to please share with me how to do it so that I can be more effective. Roy said, "You have to ask people first if they have time to talk and determine if they believe in the gospel you are sharing, because they may be of different beliefs, like Islam or Judaism or Hindu or any other religion." I responded that that was exactly why I was there sharing and hoping to talk to people who didn't believe in Jesus. Furthermore, people were moving so fast that I didn't have time to ask them if they had time to talk. It was obvious that the people were in a hurry to get into their cars and drive off.

I ended up spending half an hour talking with Roy. He was definitely confused about what he believed and did not know if Jesus was the only truth. He asked about those who were born Muslim and Hindu and who did not have any other thing to believe from birth. I assured him that we could not all be right and that one of the religions had to be the truth. He said, "What if we are all worshiping the same God, but because of our particular books and scriptures we are reaching different interpretations of who God is?" I told him that he had a valid question and I asked if he believed in the Bible. He said, "Oh, I have my Bible."

I said, "Do you read it? And have you read the Quran and seen for yourself the stuff they believe?" I realized quickly that I was talking with a cultural Christian who did not have faith and trust in Jesus. I asked him, "Roy, if you died today, would you go to heaven?"

I proceeded to explain the gospel to Roy. I told him that if I died that day, then I would go to heaven. Roy asked how I was sure of that. I told him that Jesus paid for all my past, present and future sins on the cross and, on that basis, I was sure to please God and be accepted into God's heaven. I told him that I sensed that someone had been praying for him. Roy said that his grandmother was praying for him. I ended up praying for Roy and gave him the tract he had originally refused. I also gave him my contact information and our church information. He said he was likely to come to church. I thanked him for giving me his time and he thanked me for being patient and persevering with him.

We must push beyond the façade people put up when hearing the gospel. Eighty or more percent of the people I encounter are nominal or cultural Christians who do not have real faith in Jesus and who have no relationship with God the Father. I encouraged Roy to feed his faith and spirit with the Bible that he said he had, to pray and talk to God, and to stop running from Him.

Seminary Community Outreach

Alicia Wong, a seminary student at Southwestern Baptist Theological Seminary, reported on their school door-to-door efforts under the heading "Is Door-to-Door Worth It?" published in *Biblical Woman*:

> Some of you may wonder if people even open their doors to strangers these days or give you the time to present the Gospel. They *do* open the doors, and they *do* let you share the Gospel—some neighborhoods more than others. Dr. Paige Patterson had a goal for those who lived within a one-mile radius of seminary to have the opportunity to hear the Gospel. So, from Monday to Friday the professors and students head out each day going door-to-door witnessing. The goal was reached, and the seminary is now embarking on the second mile. From all the evangelism practicum classes at SWBTS this past fall, 1,992 gospel presentations were given by 148 students, and 387 people were saved.

Door-to-door evangelism does work! As Dr. Alvin Reid stated, "In order to win lost people to Christ, we must talk to lost people."

If you share Christ with one neighbor a month, in a year 12 people will have had the opportunity to hear the gospel. If every Christian shared Christ with six neighbors to the right of them and six neighbors to the left, how different our neighborhoods would be today! Reid makes a sad observation, stating that "many Christians believe in the Good News but act as though sharing it is bad news."

There is more evidence that outreach and personal evangelism works. We all can start today without further delay and start where we are and by the grace we are given by God.

You and I are often concerned about our children and long to gather them in when they have strayed doing their own things. God the Father has His own children too and we reflect the same longing for our children as He does for His. What about God's other children to be gathered in?

12

My "Stroke" Evangelism

As we get motivated corporately in participating with the church family, we are energized at the individual level to live as witnesses of Christ in whatever state and circumstance we find ourselves. One adverse circumstance was a stroke I suffered in June 2016. I have come a long way since then and my fine motor skills for my fingers and toes are gradually coming back. It is nothing short of a miracle for my speed of recovery, and I thank God greatly.

I am getting better every day but I am still in therapy and in the gym to attain the full function of my left arm and leg, fingers and toes. I have discovered that God is with me along the way and that is the most important thing right now.

While in the hospital, I made up my mind to rejoice and to be glad in the Lord. I read the Bible, prayed always, and played lots of gospel and Christian songs. When people passed by my room, they had no doubt that there was the presence of God in the place. People would stop to ask, "What is the hope within you?" and "Why are you still smiling?" As the apostle Peter said, "[G]ive a defense to everyone who asks you a reason for the hope that is in you, with meekness and fear" (1 Peter 3:15).

Roommate 1—DM

For the first two weeks, I was alone in my room, but then a 19-year-old man was moved in as my roommate. (I will call him DM.) He had much pain from a car accident. We bonded and I developed a routine to pray with him every day, especially in the morning. We got to know our family members as they visited. He said he was raised in church but had stopped going. Because DM did not really understand the gospel, I explained it to him in many conversations.

DM had lots of young friends who would visit. They were very noisy, but I tolerated it. I would eventually quiet them down and use the time and opportunity to converse with them. I found out that many did not have a church affiliation, nor were they raised in a church-going or religious family. They thought that there was a God but they did not have a personal relationship with Him. They believed that they were basically good except for the recreational sex they indulged in, which they said was not a big deal.

Since their friend DM survived the accident, I asked them that if they had been in the same accident and had died, would they have gone to heaven? They answered in the positive because they were good people. Their answers then gave me the opportunity to explain the gospel to them. I allowed them to ask lots of questions so that it was not a one-way conversation. We must engage our youth in meaningful conversations and not be afraid of what they are thinking and the questions they are asking. I consider all these various encounters as seeds and the Holy Spirit has to take care of the growth and results.

I am encouraged by the words of Jesus: "The kingdom of God is as if a man should scatter seed on the ground, and should sleep by night and rise by day, and the seed should sprout and grow, he himself does not know how" (Mark 4:26-27). I thank God that I don't have to worry nor know how the seed sprouts and grows. Let's plant the seed.

Roommate 2—Mr. GH

DM was discharged and Mr. GH was brought in as my new roommate. Mr. GH was in his late seventies. He was a delight to be with. His pain was severe and he had limited movement due to a swollen knee. The physicians could not say exactly what was the cause of the water retention that caused so much pain. Despite his pain, he had a smile on his face and a sense of humor. We bonded quickly as we got to share and know each other. I looked forward to gleaning from his years of experience as a retired federal employee. As we shared, I got to learn of his faith journey as a young boy.

Mr. GH's grandmother used to take him to a Baptist church and he had learned some songs that he remembered. But as a grown-up, church and things of God had not been prominent in his life. I asked him that if he died that day or during this hospitalization, did he think he would be welcomed by God into His heaven? He was very honest and said he did not know. I proceeded to explain to him God's plan of salvation and why we need to put our faith in Jesus' death, burial and resurrection for the remission of our sins. Mr. GH has a heart like a child and was very receptive to the gospel. We prayed together daily and he would often ask for prayer. In one instance, he welcomed one of my guests who was led by the Spirit to pray for him. He enjoyed the Christian music I played in the room. It was hard to part with Mr. GH when he was discharged. He would not leave until we had prayed.

Mr. GH's Roommate, Mr. A

Upon my discharge, I kept in touch with Mr. GH. I would call him, and he would often call me. I would later find out that Mr. GH was readmitted to a different hospital from the one where we both received care. I visited him at the hospital and he was very glad to see me again, and we prayed together. He was then discharged.

About two months later, Mr. GH was again readmitted to the same hospital. I again visited him and bought some snacks and flowers. This time Mr. GH was heavily drugged and slept more than being awake. We conversed for a little while before he fell asleep.

While Mr. GH slept and while I waited for him to wake up so that I could say goodbye, I was led to get to know his roommate, Mr. A. Mr. A was in his late seventies, too. He was reluctant to converse but he did not have any choice because it was just me and him awake in the room. I got to know him briefly, but he did not volunteer his health condition and I did not pry. I asked Mr. A if he had a faith journey and what he believed. He was reluctant to answer my questions. I persisted and told him what awaits all of us after death and that Jesus Christ is the answer for our penalty for sin and separation from God, which results in everlasting life in hell. At this point, Mr. A got very angry. He said, "That is all good for you if that is what you believe. Just know that not everyone believes that, and people should be left alone." And that was the end of the conversation. I thanked Mr. A for allowing me to chat with him.

Shortly afterward, his son and daughter-in-law walked in. As they conversed, I learned more about his condition. Mr. A thought he would be discharged the next day, but according to his family, his condition was more serious than he was willing to admit. Sometimes, we just have to follow the leading of the Spirit to speak the word of God to people in season and out of season. I believe Mr. A has been wrestling with God and needs to be confronted with the truth before it is too late. This is what I call a divine appointment and preaching in season and out of season.

Mr. GH did not wake up before I left. I prayed for him before leaving. I greeted Mr. A and said goodbye and he actually thanked me for speaking with him. I told him that I would be praying for him. Mr. GH was later discharged, and we are still in touch.

Stroke Patients' Support Group "Church Service"

During the time I was in rehab, we had sharing sessions every Sunday in a stroke survivors support group. Stroke patients and their families were welcome to attend. We would all share about our experiences of how it happened and whether we had recognized the signs of stroke. The hospital staff coordinator of the session instructed us on stroke prevention and knowing the signs of second or subsequent strokes. We were told that there are greater chances of stroke happening again among stroke survivors. The last part of the program is what I loved the most. We were each asked to share how we were coping and what it was that was helping us cope and deal with the recovery.

For me it was an invitation to share the gospel with everyone in the group. I would tell them how my faith in God and Christ the Son was helping me cope. I would tell them that I thanked God for surviving the stroke, that I have peace always because it comes from a relationship with God, that I was not afraid of dying because I will be in heaven with Christ, that I am sure of heaven because Jesus died on the cross for all my sins, and that His rising from death gives me great hope for new life forever in eternity.

By that time, we would be having a Sunday service because those in the group who go to church would be saying "Amen."

The only thing left would have been to pass the offering plates around! I usually waited to go last so that at the end I could ask if anyone objected to me praying for the group. No one ever objected, so I would pray and close the session. Afterward, I would have further conversations with some of my fellow patients and often we would gather for lunch and talk about life and family.

I am still in touch with one of the patients, who happened to be a pastor. We are exchanging ideas on how best to reach more people for Christ, especially Muslims. He had ministered to many Muslim individuals and audiences after having pastored in a predominantly Muslim country. I had a great time in the hospital even in the midst of pain. Most of my stroke experience was good and drew me closer to Christ, who gives me strength.

Visit to the Barber Shop

Upon release from the hospital, I desperately needed a haircut. I went to the barber shop but my regular barber was busy cutting another person's hair. There was a new barber in the shop and the shop owner asked if I would allow the new barber to cut my hair. I said yes. The young man finished cutting my hair and I paid and was about to leave. He saw that I was walking with much difficulty and asked what happened. I explained that I had suffered a stroke and that I thanked God I was alive. We started talking about other things, including soccer because he was born overseas and grew up playing the game. I started to leave and he followed me outside. (I will call him Scott.)

Scott told me outside that there was something bothering him and he did not know who to speak to about it. He proceeded to pour out his heart. He was desperate and depressed. He had just found out that his wife had cheated on him and he was contemplating what to do because he could not forgive her. He said something made him feel comfortable about speaking with me. I told him that he was speaking to the right person and that I was a minister of God. From then he addressed me as Father Udo.

I told Scott that I was very sorry to hear of his betrayal and his wounded heart. I acknowledged that it must be very painful and that I could not fully understand since I had never been through this. I told Scott that he had to forgive his wife for the terrible thing she did, especially since the sexual affair was with a family friend he had trusted. The friend worked with Scott's wife in the same small business; this made the betrayal doubly difficult for Scott. He said that he had taken some initial steps and that his wife no longer worked in the same place with this guy. I applauded him for the steps he had taken. I told Scott that the only way to forgive his wife was to experience forgiveness for his own sins against God. I went on to explain the gospel to Scott and prayed with him to put his faith and trust in Jesus Christ.

There was an instant transformation that I had never experienced before. Even before I got home from the barber shop, Scott called to tell me that he had just spoken to his wife to say that he forgave her. His wife was on the phone and he wanted me to speak with her. I spoke briefly to his wife and requested that we three meet at my home the following Sunday morning but that they should attend church together before meeting with me. They both attended a Baptist church that was close to their house.

The couple and their five-year-old came to our house mid-morning that Sunday. My wife and children were all home, so I introduced them to my family. Their daughter played with my daughter while the three of us talked. Scott's wife was very remorseful for her sins and was crying. I waited for her to calm down before speaking. I encouraged them that they were on the right track, because with God nothing is impossible. Again, I explained the gospel message to them and encouraged them to put their faith in Jesus. I discovered that Scott's wife was a cultural and nominal Christian who had never understood the message of the gospel, just like her husband. I asked that they pray with me, repeating my prayer, and they both did. We spent some time together before Scott had to run to go to work. I have maintained contact with Scott and his family. For a while, I would see Scott at the barber shop and would follow up. Scott has since moved on to a different job, so I no longer see him there. But I continue to pray for Scott and his family and occasionally call him on the phone.

My Neighbors I See Almost Daily

As I said, my stroke opened doors and gave me the platform to speak to my neighbors whom I see very often. Most of them who heard of my stroke visited me in the hospital or called to express their wishes. Upon my release from the hospital, they visited me at my house. While I was in the hospital, one of my neighbors in his early forties came to visit. It was just the two of us in the room. I used the opportunity to present the gospel to him. He is a very busy businessman and never had much time in the past to talk. This time, he had the time. My stroke really got his attention. He had seen me going for regular exercise at the gym before the stroke and knew that I am a vegetarian. If a healthy person like me can have a stroke, what chance did he have, he asked himself. I explained the gospel to him and prayed with him. I asked him that if he died that day, would he see God? He said yes because he was a good person. I told him that that was not good enough. He thanked me for explaining the assurance of salvation. He said that my stroke was for him, that I took the bullet for him so that God could get his attention. I remind him of that whenever I see him.

I have spoken to many of our neighbors and have prayed with them, and there are so many stories I could tell. I just thank God for the stroke and for my neighbors, and for the opportunity to share the gospel with them. I want to see my neighbors in heaven and not just here on Earth. What about you?

Shocking the Patients with Truth

With my many therapy sessions and doctor visits, one day I got the idea of shocking people with the truth of the gospel. We have to sometimes shock people and awaken them so that they can be confronted with the gospel. After my neurologist's office visit, I got the idea of placing gospel tracts on the cars parked in the lot of the doctor's office building. This particular one said, "Where will you spend eternity?" What better time to be confronted with mortality and life than when we are focused on it? I know someone will be jolted and confronted with the truth even if they don't read the entire gospel tract. We must go out of our way and become unconventional in sharing the gospel; and as Paul would say, "See then that you walk circumspectly, not as fools but as wise, redeeming the time, because the days are evil. Therefore do not be unwise, but understand what the will of the Lord is" (Ephesians 5:17).

We must redeem the time and take advantage of every opportunity to share the gospel. If the devil was bold enough to mess with me to have a stroke, then I have decided to have him pay for it by inflicting him and his kingdom by preaching the gospel in season and out of season. I have refused to waste any of my doctor visit times, so I carry my gospel tracts with me wherever I go and am ready to share with anyone and everyone as I see an opportunity. We must be intentional about making disciples at all times. I look forward to seeing some of these patients in heaven.

Visits to the Gym and Community Centers

Part of my stroke recovery plan as made clear to me by my doctors and therapists is to continue to exercise, especially my left leg and left arm. Once I was released from the hospital, I hit the gym five days a week in addition to going to my therapy sessions. I belong to a community gym where I can visit and use any three centers that are very close to my house. I intentionally vary my visits to different locations for the purpose of sharing the gospel.

I have met lots of staff, gym members, and other people there. These include both Christians and adherents of almost all the major religions. Some of my witnessing efforts are through friendship evangelism and other efforts are just on-the-spot sharing of the gospel and giving out tracts and devotional booklets, such as *The Daily Bread*. Some of the people I see again and some I never see again. I have many memorable stories and I use my iPhone note function to record my daily gospel encounters. From time to time, I pray for the people on my encounter list.

One day I was getting ready to start exercising when a man walked in and said he was told that I play table tennis. He asked if I could go to the game room to play with him. I had planned to do exercises, but I quickly realized that this was a divine appointment. I had never played table tennis (ping pong) in this community center before and I don't remember having any discussion with anyone about it. Although I was limping, I managed to play a good game. Although the man was 83 years old, he did not look it. He had been playing ping pong for a long time and he showed me his awards for playing in senior tournaments. I ended up sharing a quick version of the gospel presentation with him and gave him a tract that said "God Is Good." I reminded him how God has been good to him by giving him good health before I left for my therapy appointment. I never saw him again.

A Muslim Woman

Another day, I went to the gym and took with me just one gospel tract titled "You Are Special." There were up to 10 people at the gym, including a young Muslim woman from the Middle

East. I had seen her a couple of times in the past. When I had tried to say hello, she had not made eye contact but had just concentrated on her exercises while listening to her music.

I said, "Lord, show me who to give this tract to." I started to exercise and after a while it was impressed on me to give the tract to the Muslim lady. I was like, "No way, Lord. You must be kidding." I didn't want to embarrass her in front of the others in the gym.

I said, "Lord, if it is for her, then let her go to the exercise equipment that is away from other people so that I can give it to her." Before I could finish my thoughts, she got up from the machine she was using and went to the ladies' room that was outside in the hallway. I took the tract from my coat pocket and went to the hallway by the water fountain to drink and wait for her. I barely drank the water and here she came. I introduced myself and told her my name. I asked for her name and she gave it to me. I tried to shake her hand, but she explained that she couldn't shake my hand because she is a Muslim. That was not going to distract me. I said to her, "Has anyone told you that you are special?" She said yes, and I said, "Yes, [calling her by her name], you are special. God said you are special." I brought out the tract and gave it to her and said to her, "You see, you are special." This was a very beautiful gospel tract with a picture of a red rose on the cover. She accepted the tract and thanked me. She entered the gym to continue her exercise.

I breathed a sigh of relief because I was very apprehensive approaching this woman, which goes to show that no matter how many times you have approached people, especially strangers and people of other cultures, there is often an uneasiness that you experience sharing the gospel. The encounter with the Muslim woman was a door-opening encounter and I believe she must have read the tract. Subsequently, I would see her occasionally at this gym. She would smile and exchange greetings. I believe God is at work in her life. We pray that God will remove the veil over her eyes so that she can see Jesus. I have not seen her lately and I pray that others would water the seed already planted through the gospel tract.

I am intoxicated by the Holy Spirit with this gospel of Jesus. It is the greatest news ever told. For me as a stroke survivor, who has been given another chance to be alive in the land of the living, it means so much to me. I do not have any other reason to be alive except for God's grace. I must use this grace that has been poured out on me for however long until I see my Jesus face to face. I will tell of His goodness as a witness until I die or until Jesus comes to rapture us up to Himself. I am enjoying it and my joy is full, proclaiming Christ crucified to all. I have many more daily gospel encounters that I don't have room to tell here.

You don't have to have a stroke to be fired up for personal evangelism, and I do not wish a stroke on you. But whatever your circumstances are—great health, poor health, in-between health, in sickness and in health, financially poor or rich—let's use it all for the glory of Jesus and be His witness wherever we are. You became a witness when you trusted and believed in Christ and the Holy Spirit of God came into your life. Your present condition or life circumstances do not change your status as a witness for Christ. A witness is a witness in all courts: high, low or supreme courts. Witnesses will testify what they see, regardless of the court and the audience. Let's do the same in all the courts of our lives.

Imagine being dragged into a court of law. Imagine you have a witness whom the judge has summoned to testify. Imagine the court is in session and the proceeding is going on. Imagine that your adversary is pressing all kinds of charges against you and will never let go. Imagine that the witness summoned by the judge knows the truth of the matter. Now imagine that the witness has refused to testify to tell what he/she knows and to speak the truth that can set you free. Would you like the witness to tell the truth in your hearing and that of the judge? Of course you would want that. You don't want the judge to slam his gavel in judgment without the witness speaking the truth. Even worse, you don't want the witness to stand and tell all kinds of stories that amuse and entertain you and at the end avoid telling the truth of the matter.

The people around us will soon face the judgment of God. It is a terrible thing to endure God's judgment because all have sinned, and no one can escape the guilty verdict. Do you really believe people will go to hell if they do not trust in Jesus as their Savior and Lord? We must continue to be witnesses of the death, burial and resurrection of Jesus Christ that saves them from the wrath of God. That is what making disciples is all about.

Yes, I hear you like I used to hear myself. You may say, "I do not have the conversational skills and wits to answer the hard questions people may throw at me." You will never have it until you engage people in gospel conversations. You already converse with your friends at work and at school. They may sometimes ask you hard questions on various topics, so it is the same except that now you are talking with a stranger. There are real fears of talking to strangers and neighbors about Christ. May I suggest you do some homework and invest in books that address the issue. One that has helped me is by Rico Tice, associate minister at All Souls Langham Place, London, who wrote the book *Honest Evangelism: How to talk about Jesus even when it's tough.*

You can google any topic on the internet and get tons of articles on them. There is so much already written and free on the internet on how to converse and have difficult conversations about the gospel. Here is one: "5 Ways to Start a Conversation About the Gospel" from jesusfilm.org or https://www.jesusfilm.org/blog-and-stories/conversation-about-gospel.html. (Hint: Try steering a conversation toward death, morality, religion, goodness or human nature.) Nothing will take away the fear until you step out in faith and tell someone about the living Christ, who will speak through you. The more you do it, the more comfortable you will feel, even if you stumble sometimes in the beginning. And being in the company of other believers and learning from real-life conversations as you go door to door is some of the best training you can get.

13

Making Disciples

Most of the presentation in this book up to this point has been on the "going" of the "go and make disciples." We must go and continue to go as a corporate body and as individual followers of Christ. As a corporate body and in addition to other ministry efforts, we must commit to at least one Sunday a month to leave the church building and go and preach to those yet to believe and yet to trust in Christ. Likewise, as individuals we must commit to individual evangelistic efforts, including friendship evangelism and any other promptings, to tell the gospel even to strangers as the Spirit of God leads. Now let's look at the rest of the command of Jesus to us, His disciples:

> Go therefore and make disciples of all the nations, bap-
> tizing them in the name of the Father and of the Son and

of the Holy Spirit, teaching them to observe all things that I have commanded you; and lo, I am with you always, even to the end of the age. (Matthew 28:19-20).

What we do is make disciples, and it is continuous, starting with going out to preach. I see three commands from Jesus: (1) New beginners/believers should be baptized; (2) they need to be taught to observe; and (3) they need to do what Jesus commanded.

A follower of Jesus should be baptized as soon as possible since it is an outward identification of the inner work God has already done in their lives. Followers of Jesus should be baptized the same way He was baptized. We should be dunked into water and be baptized in a pool or river. There are all kinds of debates about baptism: dunking or sprinkling, in whose name they should be baptized, and so forth. We need to make this as simple as we can so that the new believer can move on. To me, it is pretty clear from what Jesus said as to what name in which a new believer should be baptized. The above verse says, "baptizing them in the name of the Father and of the Son and of the Holy Spirit." What is ambiguous about "in the name of the Father, the Son and the Holy Spirit"? The beauty here is that we see the agreement and unity of the Godhead. That is what we have come to call the Trinity. Many in the book of Acts were baptized immediately upon confession of faith in Christ.

Teaching Them

We have relegated teaching to the classroom and the pulpits, and there is a place for that kind of instruction. However, making disciples is an apprenticeship process, which means learning alongside. Jesus showed us an example as He taught the disciples by doing while they watched. And they did catch on. Notice how the way the apostle Peter raised Dorcas from the dead in Acts 9:36-42 mirrored how Jesus raised Jairus's daughter from the dead in Mark 5:37-43.

There are two sides to disciple-making: teaching and observing. We have been good at teaching but not so hot about observation. That's what Jesus did with His disciples. Sometimes He sat and taught but often He taught them as they watched Him and asked questions along the way. It is the apprenticeship side that is missing from what we have been doing as a church.

Obeying and Doing the Commands

One of Jesus' first commands is to let believers know that they are witnesses, and as such, they are in the "going" business, just like the woman at the well. Let's pair up novices with more seasoned believers so that they can observe being a witness of Jesus to someone else.

May we never consign the new believers to the pews to collect dust and hope they will get up after five years of intense Bible study to live out their witnessing life. Let's remember that new believers have the same Holy Spirit that we have living in us, and as such "they can do all things through Christ" who gives them strength. They have no less of Christ than us, because they are brand-new creations just like us.

Immediately Plug New Believers into Small or Home Groups

Jesus talks about "teaching them to obey my commands" about believing in Him and loving one another. What better place than a small-group setting to obey His command? Plug the new believers into neighborhood home groups. Let them feel and touch the family of God. That's where the learning and loving take place.

I love what Bill Mowry, a veteran staff member with The Navigators, said about discipling one another. In his book *The Ways of the Alongsider: Growing Disciples Life2Life*, he wrote,

> When we minister as alongsiders, we earn the right to intentionally become involved in people's lives. Alongsiders

partner with the Holy Spirit, helping others wholeheartedly follow Jesus in all of life. We purposely do this in simple, life2life ways: loving one another, reading the Bible, telling stories, asking questions, encouraging application, and living on mission.

There are no lone rangers in the body of Christ. It is never just me and Jesus. It is always Jesus, me and His body. A fish left by itself in a fish tank will eventually die. A fish must be in its native water with other fish of its kind to grow and thrive. We need each other as disciples and followers of Christ. Iron sharpens iron.

Progressive Growth of Disciples
In Colossians 1:9-14, we see a new believer who is being prayed for by the church. We see one who is growing in the "knowledge of his will," in wisdom and understanding of the Word, and in the power to live it out by the enablement of God the Holy Spirit.

We see a growing believer who is "bearing fruit in every good work," who is strengthened along the way by the Spirit, and who is exercising endurance and patience throughout the difficulties of life. The growth culminates in the giving of joyful thanks always to our Father God. The growth is also reflected in apostle Peter's letter to believers in 2 Peter 1:65-7. We grow from faith to moral excellence, knowledge, self-control, patient endurance, godliness, brotherly love, and love for all people.

The Great Commission as Recorded by Mark
Although we have focused on Matthew's recording of the Great Commission, we also need to heed Mark's account:

Later He appeared to the eleven as they sat at the table; and He rebuked their unbelief and hardness of heart, because they did not believe those who had seen Him after He had risen. And He said to them, "Go into all the world and preach the Gospel to every creature. He who believes and is baptized will be saved; but he who does not believe will be condemned. And these signs will follow those who believe: In My name they will cast out demons; they will speak with new tongues; they will take up serpents; and if they drink anything deadly, it will by no means hurt them; they will lay hands on the sick, and they will recover." (Mark 16:14-18)

Why would Jesus give His disciples this command after rebuking them for unbelief and hardness of heart? You would think that at this point this would disqualify the disciples from even being considered for such an important assignment. Jesus had to rebuke them so they can believe Him and become true disciples. An unbeliever in Christ is not a disciple. Our unbelief /doubt cannot stop God from doing what He has already determined we will do. He will give us the power to believe and to do His commands. So please stop saying, "I have not spoken to people before about Jesus." He will enable you to do so now if you are willing. Likewise, don't say, "Oh, we have never gone out as a congregation before to tell our neighbors about Christ. Even so we have never used a Sunday in place of a regular church service to go and be a witness to our church neighbors." Just because most churches have never done so, that doesn't mean it cannot be done.

Now note the particulars of Mark's account. I assume that making disciples and preaching the gospel are one and the same. Without the preaching, there is no making of disciples. We must start with the telling of who Jesus is. Let people encounter Jesus and first be saved. We can never avoid the go and the going of the gospel. Notice that it says to preach to every creature. I take it to mean every living person without exception. We must go to all and knock on every door and on every heart.

Let us also note that Mark records the results of the preaching and the consequences. Those who believe are saved from the wrath of God. Those who refuse to believe condemn themselves to judgment and His wrath. It is that simple. We are not playing games here; this is serious business of everlasting consequences. We must take this commission seriously. It is why people like apostle Paul breathed and lived every minute for preaching the gospel. "That I may win all to Christ" was his motto. Hell is true and real. Do you believe in hell?

Signs and Wonders

Some who delight in declaring what God can and can no longer do would love that I skip this part of the Commission. It says, "And these signs will follow those who believe: In My name they will cast out demons; they will speak with new tongues; they will take up serpents; and if they drink anything deadly, it will by no means hurt them; they will lay hands on the sick, and they will recover."

The signs are to follow all believers of all times: past, present and future. It was for the first disciples and every other disciple who believes since Christ gave the promise. There is no need to pray if there is no expectation from God to act.

I believe the promise of signs was given in the context of the "go and preach the gospel." If we are not going, then why should we expect any signs? The signs are there for the unbelieving to see and turn to Jesus. As we are obedient to the preaching and telling, we will see the miracles happen. The signs are never the focus but rather outgrowth from the going and making disciples. No wonder most recent miracles are happening in places where the gospel is being preached! Many missionaries going from the West and preaching in foreign lands are seeing miracles and signs they never experienced in America or in Europe. God is still the same everywhere the gospel is being preached to the unbelieving.

Many today are pounding their pulpits and expecting miracles and signs. May I suggest that we go to where the unbelieving are, preach to them, and *then* expect and experience the signs just as the early apostles did? This doesn't mean that Jesus will not answer any prayers of faith prayed in the church building, but signs definitely follow when the gospel is preached to the unbelieving.

I am reminded of a recent testimony by a Western missionary who covers North Africa and the Middle East. He recounted the miracle of Christ in saving a Muslim man that happened about a year ago. A single lady in their Cairo office was taking a taxi cab to another part of town. She entered the cab and the driver was obviously a Muslim with his long and full beard. The man had a *zebibah*—a mark on the forehead that one gets from repeatedly pounding one's head on the prayer mat during Muslim prayers. The lady heard the small voice of the Holy Spirit say, "Tell the cab driver that Jesus loves him." She was like, "No way. God, you have the wrong person." The voice continued to speak and she started to negotiate with God, finally telling Him, "I will say that to the driver at the end of my ride. I will pay the driver, open the door, and before I close the door I will tell him that Jesus loves him." Scared and frightened, that is exactly what she did.

The young lady got to her destination, paid the cab driver and, before closing the door, said to him that Jesus loves him. She closed the door of the taxi and started running. The cab driver got out of his cab and ran after her. He told her to stop and she did. The driver then told her that for the past two weeks, Jesus had been appearing to him at night. The last night, Jesus told him that a young lady would enter his cab, tell him that Jesus loved him, and would close the door and start running away. He said he was expecting what had just happened. They walked back to the cab and, sitting in the back seat, she led him to Christ and prayed with him. A week later, the former Muslim was baptized.

Now that is a miracle and a sign. We are all being called to simple obedience and trust in Christ. The voice of the Holy Spirit will continue to speak to all believers. May we hear and obey His voice regardless of where we are and who we are with.

14

Watching the Back Doors

When a congregation has been losing members year after year and net outflow and inflow is in the negatives, you would think someone should notice. There is a big hemorrhage in the house. The back door is wide open and no one is watching who is leaving and why they are leaving. This entire book has been dedicated to calling us into intentional action in the going of the "go and make disciples." However, what good is it in being energized to evangelize and bring people to Christ if they come to church and subsequently leave unnoticed through the back door?

The Sad Statistics
Ryan Sheehan says, in his article published in *The Christian Post* and titled "3,500 Leave the Church Every Day":

There is an ongoing silent migration away from the church of an estimated 3,500 individuals each and every day. A 2014 study indicated that over 1.2 million people will leave the church in the next year. Several factors are contributing to this trend, but the majority of individuals who are leaving the church report that they no longer feel connected. Can this be reversed? Can the church connect with people before it is too late?

Part of making disciples is also making sure we are connecting with people. When we are not making the connections and there are no authentic relationships, people get discouraged and leave the church. Many reasons have been documented for why people are leaving the church. Many books have been written on this subject of people leaving and quitting church; so, my intent here is to call our attention to the subject. One of the best I have read is by Julia Duin in her 2008 book *Quitting Church: Why the Faithful Are Fleeing and What to Do About It.*

What she said is that people must feel they belong and can add value to doing and being church. They get discouraged and leave because they feel unemployed or underemployed. One good way to deal with that is to get everyone doing what Jesus told us to do: Go and make disciples. There is no greater excitement and joy than being part of what God is already doing in peoples' lives. There is great joy in heaven over one sinner who repents, and so there is also great joy here among followers of Christ. Remember, we are just a link in the chain that God is using to draw us and others to Himself. We plant and water and God gives the increase and the growth.

The Casual Acquaintances

People are bound to leave the church and get disappointed if all we offer them is a 30-minute Sunday sermon and two minutes of interaction in the church foyer. Often it is even less than two minutes! Most often, the church regulars greet one another and spend time catching up about the previous week. Guess who is left out? The newcomer and visitor. I have seen newcomers and visitors dash out the door because of this.

When we begin to be and do church right, we all will be involved in witnessing, and newcomers and visitors will have had a connection to at least two people in the congregation before they show up on Sundays. The pair who shared the gospel with them would most likely be looking out for the first-timer who recently put their trust in Jesus.

The problem of ignoring visitors happens both in big and small church congregations. Recently, a friend shared how she and her children visited a church of about 60 people. You would think a church of that size would notice the only visitors of the day, but that is not what happened. At the dismissal, the regulars went into their various cliques to talk and chat. After an awkward five to ten minutes, my friend and her children decided to leave since no one stopped by to say hello to the only visitors on that Sunday. It was on their exit at the door that a lady waved and said goodbye. What a horrible, cold church encounter.

Again, I still point to the necessity of the church being all we are designed to be and making the gospel our primary business. If a small congregation of 60 people made the gospel their priority, then someone would have paid attention to this family. Someone would have approached them to welcome them and be friendly. Someone would have asked about the visitors' faith journey, if they are believers or not, or if they are looking for a church home. Someone would have discovered how best to follow up with my friend and her children if they had been seeking a relationship with Christ. Thank God, my friend is a believer in Christ and follower of Jesus. But they will never show up at that church again. How sad that would have been if they were seeking to know Christ.

The "One-Anothers"—Care Monitors and Ministers

The Gospels and especially the epistles are full of the instructions for caring for one another. Here are few examples:

> For you, brethren, have been called to liberty; only do not use liberty as an opportunity for the flesh, but through love serve one another (Galatians 5:12).

> Be kindly affectionate to one another with brotherly love, in honor giving preference to one another (Romans 12:10).

> No one has seen God at any time. If we love one another, God abides in us, and His love has been perfected in us (1 John 4:12).

The best context of caring for one another is in small groups. People get lost in the big crowd. It is hard to know that someone is sick in the big crowd when they are not connected with a small group. We must take small or home groups seriously and find ways to place people in one as soon as they join a congregation. There should be ongoing lives lived and shared within small groups. It should be organic and not made up or forced. We should know when one is suffering so that all may suffer along. Likewise, when there is rejoicing, all can rejoice and celebrate together.

Some churches have care centers and people on staff to manage and coordinate such efforts. That is ideal. But where there are no staff people, a volunteer should be put in charge of such. Whether with a paid staff member or a volunteer, a team of church members should be formed to oversee the caring and visitation ministry. Visits to shut-ins and people in the hospital should be made by all, not just the pastors, care team, or care leaders. We are all in this together.

The burden and responsibility are on all of us. If we are aware of any in need in the body of Christ, then we should pray for them and do something. First, let others in the church know so that they can have the opportunity to serve one another. Sometimes we may have to ask permission from the person needing help before we can share with others, but in many cases, we do not.

When you are lying in a hospital bed alone, that is when you really appreciate the body of Christ. I was hospitalized for more than two months after my stroke and I saw the "one another" in action. The body of Christ really showed up and showered me with love and care. Our home group looked out for my family, brought food, and checked up on us on a regular basis. This was during the summer and one of the brothers in my home group took it on himself to mow my lawn.

Unfortunately, that is not the story of everyone in the church. Some people have had some horrible experiences. They were sick and no one visited or called. Our care for one another extends to all aspects of our lives, such as job seeking and support during periods of unemployment, other emergency situations, etc. We must be there for one another. After all, membership in the body of Christ should have its privileges too.

Let's learn from those who walk the walk and improve on how best to care for one another, especially new believers and followers of Christ. We must keep our eyes open to the back door and be aware of the needs around us and, by Christ's enabling, meet those needs. Will people occasionally leave a body of believers? Yes, but let the departures be the exception instead of the norm. There are many reasons why people leave a congregation. I encourage leaders to find out why. Let's not pay lip service to what people are saying but address the issues in small-group settings or even with the entire church body. Every family has issues, and the body of Christ is no exception.

Small/Home-Group Formation

We have established the need for ministry in the body of Christ. We must care for one another and that is really evidence of us belonging to Christ (see 1 John 4:12). But how do we get people into living life together the best we can in our present generation of city, suburban and country-style living? We are not living in the same or similar arrangements of the people before us as illustrated in the book of Acts and in the epistles. It is much easier to live and care for one another when we are living in close proximity. So how can we bridge the gap and not use our scattered living arrangements as an excuse for not caring for one another? Of course, we have technology that the early church did not have. We have cars, smart phones, Facebook pages, and other social media that should help us keep in touch. We must have a way to organize ourselves in small groups to make the one-another commands possible in our present church arrangements.

We may see each other in the Sunday morning worship service but, as we have acknowledged, that is not enough, nor is it sufficient to maintain meaningful relationships. Our busy schedules compound our problem of doing church and doing life together as brothers and sisters in Christ. The busyness is not just difficult work schedules and long-distance commutes but also a new enemy of our time: social media. We are spending ridiculous hours on social media, which feeds our sin of self-absorption and self-love.

How does a church organize its members into logical, organic and meaningful relational small/home groups? This is the million-dollar question; but the intent here is not to solve it but to bring it to light as an important component and tool for making disciples. A new baby or existing babies must be cared for in the family. The new believers and the existing believers need to be in small groups. How do we get each to where it may be appropriate for them? In many churches, announcements are made about joining an existing small/home group. Most times, people do not even pay attention to such announcements. They are saying, "You should thank God I showed up on Sunday morning, so don't expect me to be in any other gathering for the rest of the week." But without small groups, the congregation dies.

What is a small/home group within a church congregation? How do you go about forming one? A good article on forming a successful home group is titled "How to Successfully Launch a Holistic Small Group (cell group) Ministry" by Randall Neighbour, ministry president of Transforming Others Under Christ's Hands (TOUCH). He says to "think organism, not organization." Neighbour further says that "a healthy HSG ministry must grow slowly and take on a life of its own for it to become a permanent new way of life for the members of the group and your church." In other words, have a working prototype before replicating. He says that pastors and church leaders must lead by example by starting a HSG themselves and also visiting other churches that have healthy HSGs that are impacting lives.

Many people have written on this subject of home-group formation and there are tons of books on this subject. Churches must make them a top priority if they are going to retain all these new disciples. The last thing you want to see happen is for people to meet Christ through your church and then for those people to wander off after not getting their needs met or when they feel abandoned.

If we are looking for transformation and a major change in paradigm, we need leaders who are committed to changing certain fundamental practices of the church. Small groups are key to a successful local body of Christ.

15

A Need for Fearless Leaders of the Gospel

In the broadest sense, every believer and follower of Jesus is a leader. Any of us can and should lead people to Christ. For us to be fearless leaders, we must love God and fear Him. When we know who it is who speaks, we fear Him and no longer fear mere mortals. We have become leaders who fear the people and have no fear of God. Oswald Chambers said, "[T]he remarkable thing about fearing God is that when you fear God, you fear nothing else, whereas if you do not fear God you fear everything else." "Blessed is everyone that feareth the Lord" (Psalm 128:1 KJV).

Pastors are afraid of the congregation and also of bullying elders and board members. Pastors think they must always answer to the board/elders because they have control of their paychecks.

Who has called you to lead, if I may ask? If God called, then to God alone we must answer.

The spread of the gospel has suffered due to the immense fear of church leaders; this fear has been passed on to the congregation. If we are going to make a big paradigm shift and lead the church into a new era of making the gospel the main business of the church and its priority, then we need fearless leaders who obey God and leave the consequences to God. We are not advocating for renegade pastors and leaders. We are calling for leadership that works together by putting God's interests above their interests, positions and titles.

My experience of being an elder/board member of two different churches in the Washington, DC, area has taught me that we must do church leadership differently and boldly. We are catering to our own voices and the popular voices of the people, which may not be the voice of God. In one church during board meetings, evangelism was not even discussed. We were most concerned about having enough money to meet payroll, maintain the building from leaks, and pay for the landscaping. We were more concerned with the outward appearance of the building than with the people who were inside the building.

In another church, we talked about evangelism and tried to do it. However, our motive was sometimes wrong. We were more concerned with the number of people attending the church than anything else. More attendance amounted to more tithes and offerings, and for our struggling church, we were successful if we paid our rent! We were always hoping that at the end of the month we would have enough. We were more interested in exciting growth strategies, such as the Purpose-Driven Life fad. Our focus was misdirected; it was "bring people into the building, dead or alive."

We did some good and there were instances where people would encounter Jesus in these churches but it was not from well-thought-out intentional evangelism. Many of the people who attended as visitors were clearly transplants from other churches within the Washington metro area. Most new people were already believers who had just moved into the area from another city, state or even other countries.

We were sometimes but not always intentional about going out and making disciples. We were shackled by our church structure and leadership styles instead of relying on the boldness of the Holy Spirit. It is time we own up and accept that our leadership style is not working and that we need to lead in a different way, with different priorities and new results. We need leaders with the boldness of the Spirit to dismantle the current church structure of being inwardly focused and church-building focused. We do not need more elders and board members who think our work is solely to take care of the church building and raise funds to maintain it.

We must learn from those who have gone before us. We have so many examples in the Bible. Starting with Abraham, God told Joseph, Moses, David, Isaiah, Jeremiah, the Virgin Mary and others, "Do not fear." Do you think we know better than God when it comes to fear? He knows we humans are fearful; so, He says, "Do not fear." Some counted and said there is close to 365 commands of "Do not fear" in the Bible – one for each day.

Isaiah

When we hear the voice of God like Isaiah did, we are humbled. We must then speak and let the chips fall where they may. In Isaiah 6:1-5, Isaiah heard the voice of God and was terrified and humbled. Isaiah did not have any choice in saying yes when God asked, "Whom shall I send, and who will go for Us?" Isaiah said, "Here am I! Send me." It was not a popular message that Isaiah had to deliver to a rebellious Israel. It is the same message of the gospel and is not popular today. Are you ready to take the radical and transforming idea of using at least one Sunday a month to go door to door to its logical end so that you can transform the way you do and are church? What will your members think? Well, they don't belong to you; they are not your members. The people belong to God. The people in church are looking for strong leaders who will hear God and lead them to God by example. The people will follow when they know leaders are hearing God and are willing to obey Him.

Deborah, a Judge and Prophetess, and Jael, a Housewife

When Israel was doing their own thing and God gave them over to their enemies, they cried out to God, who then appointed courageous "Deborah, a prophetess, the wife of Lappidoth" to lead the people. When Barak, commander of the Israeli army, was reluctant to go fight the enemy, Deborah inspired the people and said, "I will surely go with you; nevertheless, there will be no glory for you in the journey you are taking, for the LORD will sell Sisera into the hand of a woman." God gave a decisive victory to Israel, and Sisera, the commander of the enemy army, was struck dead by another courageous woman of God, Jael. (Read the entire account in Judges 4 and 5.) God is using all (regardless of age or gender) who are fearless, available, and willing to inspire God's people to do His work.

Jeremiah

In Jeremiah 1:4-10, Jeremiah was told, "I ordained you a prophet to the nations." We also have been called by Jesus to go from Jerusalem to Judea to Samaria and to all the world to proclaim His gospel. Like Jeremiah, we all have similar reasons why we cannot go, such as being too young or too old, or we cannot speak eloquently. God did not buy those reasons then and He is not buying them now. He has filled us with His Holy Spirit, who will speak for us if we make ourselves available.

Notice the agricultural theme for Jeremiah's assignment. It is "to root out and to pull down, to destroy and to throw down, to build and to plant." All of these sound like tough jobs and hard work that require boldness of the Spirit to do. We are to "root" the Word of God and "uproot" sin and traditions that stop people from seeing God. We are to build and plant the Word. God is not talking about building church buildings.

Our beautiful church edifices are seen as a sign of success. We build people for the kingdom of God. We are to do all these without being afraid. Jeremiah was instructed, "Do not be afraid of their faces." If we look at the feedback from people (or their negative emails), then we will not do anything for God. Rather, let's turn to the face of Jesus, the author and finisher of our faith.

Mary Magdalene and the Other Mary:
First Missionaries of the Newborn Church

The church was born upon the resurrection of Jesus. Separately at the empty tomb, an angel and the risen Christ said to Mary Magdalene and the other Mary, "Do not be afraid. Go and tell My brethren [the disciples]" (Matthew 28:1-10). These courageous women worshiped Jesus, obeyed Him, and did not continue to cling to Him so that the gospel could go forward.

Apostle Paul

The apostle Paul was not afraid of preaching the gospel even while in prison. When he felt afraid at some point, God assured him, "Do not fear." Paul's joy was that the gospel was preached. Is that our joy today?

In Philippians 1:12-18, Paul pleads that, above all else, the gospel be preached. I don't think he is telling the people that when you gather together, preach to one another. The preaching was done outside to those who needed to hear. He was calling for all of God's people because the letter was read to all the people in the church. Everyone was involved, not just a select few.

Later in the chapter, Paul referred to adversaries who were within and without. The real adversary is Satan himself, who would not like us to work together for the advancement of the gospel. Satan will use some church leaders and church people to quench the spirit of the gospel. We must stand fast in one spirit, standing together in one mind and contending and striving for the gospel.

If Paul, while in prison, was still leading the church to advance the gospel, then what is our excuse these days? Not only was he leading and encouraging the church, but Paul was also preaching the gospel in captivity. He preached to the palace guards who were assigned to watch him and were chained to him under house arrest. Many of our brothers and sisters are in prison in many countries of the world for preaching the gospel. Those of us in "free" countries, where the doors to the gospel have not yet been shut, should do all we must do to spread the gospel, person to person and door to door.

Paul says, "My chains are in Christ; and most of the brethren in the Lord, having become confident by my chains, are much more bold to speak the word without fear." Let's be encouraged by the sufferings of people like Paul who have gone before us, and also of our brothers and sisters currently in prison around the world, and become bold and fearless to preach the gospel. The gospel is worth dying for at all cost. Let's preach it before we die.

Timothy: An apprenticeship in Fearless Leadership
Paul groomed Timothy in leadership and had a succession plan. We must also train and groom the next generation of fearless

leaders who must carry the gospel beyond where we can currently go. In Philippians 2:19-24, Timothy was trained to looked for "the things which are of Christ Jesus." He had seen Paul sacrifice all things for the sake of Christ. Can the next generation see our sacrifices for the gospel? Or are they seeing our perks and privileges—our nice homes, travel, and lush expense accounts? Are we leaders who are said to "sincerely care for your state," referring to the people of God? We care for God's people by equipping them to reach their maximum potential for God and to accomplish His mandate to "go and make disciples." Of course, God will provide and take care of His servant leaders when we take care of His kingdom business.

Paul wrote later in 2 Timothy to not fear, to be strong in the Lord, to endure hardship, to preach the gospel in season and out of season, and to fulfill the ministry.

From Paul to Titus: Another Apprenticeship in Fearless Leadership

"Speak these things, exhort, and rebuke with all authority. Let no one despise you," says Titus 2:15. It cannot be any clearer than that. These words do not sound like words for the wimpy. You cannot be afraid if you are to exhort and rebuke. These are what fearless leaders do. They exhort but they also rebuke with all authority in Christ. Let's rebuke ourselves for the way we have neglected our primary mission of "go and make disciples." Let's not sugarcoat it any longer. What we are doing is not working. Will people despise us when we call for change? Yes. The instruction here is to just ignore them. We don't fight back; we let God fight for us for we have heard the clear voice of God say, "Go and make disciples."

Apostle Peter: A Fearless Leader Restored and Reinstalled

Peter was restored to lead. Is this where we are today? We all have been there and need restoring. God is restoring and empowering us to lead His church again. Read the account of Jesus' encounter with Peter in John 21:15-17.

Jesus wants us to succeed in the mission He has given us. He is encouraging us as He did with Peter. Jesus said, "Peter, do you love Me?" And I would add "more than these?" The "more than these" are the many fish (other activities) we are catching (involved in) instead of being the fishers of men and women for which we have been ordained from the foundation of the world. We can easily lose focus just like Peter.

Jesus is saying to you and me, "Feed My lambs," "Tend My sheep," and "Feed My sheep." Notice the progression. First are the lambs who need to be birthed into the kingdom through the power of the gospel that is preached. We must first catch the lambs and carry them to where they can be fed. These are definitely new believers who have recently put their faith and trust in Christ. We must also tend the sheep by teaching them and allowing them to learn through observation and apprenticeship.

Notice the emphasis on "My." The sheep, the body of Christ, the church, belong to Jesus without any question. Jesus paid the highest price for His sheep. There is no greater sacrifice we can perform than what Jesus already accomplished on the cross. Jesus is looking for bold leaders who are not afraid to help gather His sheep into His fold. It calls for boldness and leadership like we have never seen in our century.

Confronting What Exists Today

There are so many churches that started off as independent churches that have now become chains. Often these churches were started by one man or woman who had a good vision. They have now become so big that they have their general overseers (GOs), bishops and many other pastors answering to their hierarchy. The men and women at the top of the hierarchy have often become powerful and feared by the subordinate pastors and congregation members.

I heard a friend once say that the people now fear the words of their GOs or bishops more than they fear the words of God. There is abnormal worship and reverence for some of these men/women of God. They themselves may not be aware of it, but it is real. I would hate to think that they know and enjoy the inordinate worship and bowing down by mere humans like them. I realize that what is proposed in this book would not have a day in court of implementation at the lowest individual congregational levels of some of these churches without the GO's/bishop's/pope's approval. Unless the GOs/bishops/popes sign off on this plan, you cannot see transformation of the nature as proposed in this book in such churches.

I was told that a local pastor cannot use at least one Sunday a month for going out to preach the gospel because he answers and takes orders from the regional lead pastor, who in turn takes orders from the state lead pastor, who in turn takes orders from the GO/bishop/Pope at the headquarters. What will it take to break the shackles of tradition in these churches with such hierarchical organizational structures? I don't know, but with God all things are possible. What will it take for the Catholic, Lutheran, Methodist, Baptist and other major denominations to uproot their traditions? In most of these denominations, the pastors do not just answer to the local elders and board; they also have to toe the lines of the denominational decrees from their popes and bishops. I am imagining and praying for the day when God will have His way in these churches so that the people of God will be released to fulfill Christ's mandate to make disciples.

I believe that there will be some bold local pastors who may venture out against the grain of tradition. I am believing for all God's churches to be mobilized for going out to make disciples for Christ. I envision the day when the Catholic church would equip and mobilize members of their congregations for going out to preach the gospel to the glory of God.

I am making a bold call to these general overseers, bishops, popes and denominational superintendents, presidents of various church conventions such as the Southern Baptist Convention, and any other powers that may be to adopt the proposals in this book and allow the local churches to implement them for the sake of Christ. Nothing is impossible, and God can speak to His servants who are willing to listen.

Leadership in Para-church Organizations for the Gospel

We must use all para-church organizations to propagate the gospel. They have done lots of good, but it is time to move to the new phase of focus. It is not enough to have the mass gatherings to teach and encourage the people. The people must be led into going and making disciples. Those conference halls are full in most part because we have people who do not often know or are searching for their real purpose for living and are looking for direction. The para-church leaders must inspire and help lead these people and all believers to one purpose: to do the work assigned to us from the beginning of the world.

It will take bold leaders to step up to this new stage by co-ordinating with local churches and taking advantage of the mass gatherings to go into the streets to share the gospel. It will take sacrifice and preference for Christ to accomplish what is proposed here. These leaders must sacrifice their what-is-in-it-for-me-and-my-organization mentality. I am thinking of orga-nizations and leaders, such as the Joyce Meyers Ministries, that attract such huge crowds. There are many of these leaders who have conferences nationally and internationally. Let them engage the believers to go to their neighbors and townspeople to preach the gospel.

Let's Confront Our Fears

One of the songs I have fallen in love with lately is by the group Casting Crowns. Casting Crowns has a new song born out of an encounter with cancer by the leader of the group. The song's refrain says,

> Oh my soul, you are not alone.

> There's a place where fear has to face the God you know.

When will your fear of whatever is tormenting you face the God you know? It is either that your fear is bigger than the God you know or that your God is bigger than the fear you face right now. Take your fear to God in prayer right now. We must call our fears by name and face them squarely. We must confront our fears and the weights and sins that beset us. Like the writer of Hebrews wrote:

> Therefore, we also, since we are surrounded by so great a cloud of witnesses, let us lay aside every weight, and the sin which so easily ensnares us, and let us run with endurance the race that is set before us, looking unto Jesus, the author and finisher of our faith, who for the joy that was set before Him endured the cross, despising the shame, and has sat down at the right hand of the throne of God. (Hebrews 12:1-2)

Those brave and fearless leaders who went before us are watching and cheering us on. They are our fellow witnesses for Christ and His truth. We must run as they ran. They ran as martyrs and most were martyred. There are, however, the weights and sins that stand in our way. The weights may even be the good things we have been doing, maybe even the traditions of our church that hinder us. Let's also accept that there are some sins among us and repent of them. The weights and sins must go. We must run free of fear and run to Jesus, the One who chose and called us to the relationship and to the race.

There is a need for endurance that produces character to lead. There are risks in following Christ and we must take the risks for Christ to lead people to Jesus. We must also accept the shame and ridicule of leading people to Jesus. There is shame to be suffered when people mock what we are doing and our desire to propagate the gospel. There will be condescending laughter even in the church when people hear the idea of using at least one Sunday a month to go and preach the gospel. There will be shame to be suffered knocking door to door to tell people about the love of Jesus. This is nothing compared to the shame and humiliation suffered by our Lord Jesus for us on the cross. The cross is the worst death and humiliation for One who did not do anything worthy of being crucified on the cross.

There is also a great joy to look forward to that fuels us to run and take anything hurled against us. There is the joy of being with God forever and of hearing, "Well done, good and faithful servant. You were faithful over a few things; I will make you ruler over many things. Enter into the joy of your Lord."

There is the joy experienced now as we obey the commands to go and make disciples. There is partying in heaven over one sinner who repents. We join in that party right now and right here. There is no greater joy than telling someone about the love of Jesus and seeing their life transformed by the power of the gospel.

Whether you see the transformation immediately or not, there is still great joy in obeying the command of Jesus. Is it possible that many lack joy because they are not participating in the joy of heaven and partying with the angels? Many in the church may be seeking only the worldly party with their friends here and so are missing the party of heaven.

There is the joy of being with God our Father forever. It is our greatest joy that our names are written in the book of life.

Make Your Argument and Case to Christ

The summary of what I have proposed is to mobilize all followers of Christ and to use at least one Sunday a month to go out to the neighbors to pray for them and tell them of the love of Christ and the good news of His gospel of salvation. By doing so, the church body will be revived and rejuvenated. The individual members will be discipled and trained and will joyfully participate in one-on-one evangelism wherever they live, go and be. Even if you dismiss what has been proposed in this book, please participate in the following simple exercise.

Please take a chair and place it in the middle of the room. Pretend that our Lord Jesus is sitting on that chair. Now look toward the chair. Begin to recite all your arguments and reasons why you think the idea proposed in this book cannot be done. Record your words so that you can listen to yourself later. Also listen to what you believe Jesus would say to you after hearing your arguments and reasons.

Go further and list for Jesus your own ideas of how you can obey His command to go and make disciples that will engage all the people in the congregation and motivate them to personal evangelism. Listen again to what Jesus would say. Now go and do what you have said.

I am only a messenger and have done my duty to deliver that which I have received. May the Lord bless you as you obey Jesus' command to go and make disciples. I look forward to seeing you in heaven. And let's bring as many as we can to heaven with us.

16

Questions and Objections

There are legitimate questions. We appreciate all views and have done the best to address them.

Q: What is the alternative to what you propose?

The alternative is to do nothing, to stay in the church building, to continue the party, to feel comfortable in the status quo, and to just take care of each other in the "clubhouse." It is insanity to continue to do the same thing but expect a different result. How long can the church sustain the status quo? I get the sense that if we do not willingly change, God will use other means to get us out of the clubhouse. He may use persecution, which has always worked in the past to spread the gospel. Look at the early church. God scattered and dispersed them from Jerusalem into the other regions. Around the world and in my native country, ISIS, Boko Haram and other similar terrorist organizations have targeted gatherings in church buildings. Look at some of the church shootings happening in the United States. When this happens, many may be fearful and stop coming to the church building. Believers will be forced to live out their faith and preach the gospel from their homes or wherever they go.

Q: What about the effectiveness of door-to-door evangelism?

Some will argue that it is not effective going door to door to preach the gospel. They point to the Jehovah's Witnesses (JW) and the questions such an approach raises. First, the JWs do not have the patent on going door to door. It was Jesus' idea as He sent His disciples. If both the JWs and the Mormons, neither of whom have the truth, are doing what Jesus said, then how much more should we, who have the true Jesus, be doing so? The JWs and the Mormons have been ineffective not because of the method but because of the false message of a different Jesus Christ. They both deny the deity of Christ, so God cannot grant them success in spreading falsehood and converting people to a false god.

As to the effectiveness, let Jesus be the judge. It worked then, and it will work now when the gospel is proclaimed.

Q: What about going to knock on doors of total strangers? How can that be effective when you have not established a relationship with them?

Yes, we will meet total strangers. When did Jesus say we should only preach to people we know? Yes, there's a place for friendship evangelism if it's properly done and if the gospel is eventually presented to the friend. However, when we approach anyone and present the gospel, it speaks for itself. The Spirit of Jesus is the gospel and He speaks and brings conviction. We do not bring conviction—only the Holy Spirit does.

Also, when Jesus sent His disciples out, the Bible tells us that they went from village to village preaching. There's no indication that the disciples had relationships with all the people of these villages. They may have become acquainted with some but certainly not the entire village.

When we knock on doors, it is Jesus Himself knocking at the doors of people's hearts and minds. Jesus Christ already knows these people and has been working with them before we ever show up at their doors. They may not know us and we may be total strangers, but they can't deny knowing God their creator (see Romans 1:20-21).

Q: Is there any room for flexibility or is it door to door and nothing else?

The preferred strategy for implementation is door to door because it is on Sunday and it is the same time or close to the same time as existing church services. We are talking about mid-morning to early afternoon. Most people are at home, so what better place to meet them than at their homes? However, there can be combinations of other methods or target areas. Based on the understanding of your community, a church can go to where they think they can reach more people. It can be a shopping mall or people on the street or special events in the community, such as carnivals. The whole concept is to use the critical Sunday gathering time when we have the most church resources (people). Again, the goal is not to call for another separate going-out event for church members in addition to the Sunday morning service.

The same concept applies when implementing this idea at small/home-group settings. The going-out should always be in place of regularly scheduled meetings. The small/home groups have more flexibility to change their day and time of going out. For example, if small/home-group meetings are on Friday night from 6 p.m. on, then they can decide to go out on a Saturday or another day and time when they can reach more people.

Q: What about using the time for other church outreach programs?

I have heard about outreach programs such as going to the community to help out with cleaning and repairing of people's homes or other helpful activities. Some churches are already doing that. We commend all good works done for Christ. The danger of such works is that our primary objective of preaching the gospel is not stated upfront and recipients or benefactors of our kindness may think of us as having ulterior motives. It is fine as long as the intent (that the gospel will be presented) is made known at some point in the process. Otherwise, it is just as good as any other social club doing good work for the community. That is the idea behind the "social gospel": to just do good with no strings attached. There are lots of good works that don't transform people because the power of the gospel of Christ is missing and was never presented.

Whenever other going-out activities are embraced by a church, we must make sure that the gospel is preached. There are examples of ministries that feed and clothe the poor while they present the gospel to people. These ministries state clearly that preaching the gospel is their goal. Of course, there are exceptions in meeting people's needs in disaster and other emergency situations. In those cases, we just meet needs, period, and Christ will do the rest.

Q: Isn't it possible that many will not come to church if they know in advance of a scheduled gospel going-out Sunday?

Yes, it's true that many will skip church service on those days, but for how long? I believe it is part of the process of separating the sheep from the goats. Maybe they never belonged to Christ, in which case they now have another opportunity to choose Christ and answer His call. If they continue to skip the gospel going-out events, then they will eventually stop coming to church or go to another congregation that has no demands to obey the Great Commission. Let them go, and pray for them. Pastors and ministry leaders must give accounting of people under their teaching and care. I would rather preach the truth and obey Christ than placate people in the pews while they are on their way to hell sitting in church. This is the hard truth that must be told.

Q: Won't this plan mess up the order in the church?

That's exactly the point. It is intended to mess up the current church order and establish an old new way of being and doing church. The current order can no longer be sustained. We need a new order where we all become a going-out church, not just trapped inside a building every Sunday.

Q: Won't it be embarrassing and won't people feel ashamed going out into the neighborhoods?

"Therefore, whoever confesses Me before men, him I will also confess before My Father who is in heaven. But whoever denies Me before men, him I will also deny before My Father who is in heaven" (Matthew 10:32-33). We have trained Christ's followers to be afraid to take risks for God. Everyone wants to be safe in the church. We are good "closet" Christians. It is time to come out. Even the LGBTQ community members are boldly coming out of their closets, so why not us?

Q: What if the people haven't been trained?

Once you encounter Jesus, you become a disciple and evangelist in essence. Jesus is asking for witnesses. Case in point: The woman at the well experienced Jesus, fell in love with Him, and immediately went to her village to tell everyone. You don't need people to go to Bible school in order to say, "Come and see the Savior and Messiah." What is our excuse? We know more than the woman at the well in terms of Bible knowledge.

Q: Doesn't the Bible say to forsake not the assembly of one another, and Sunday is for that purpose?

Great try and good objection! First, Sunday is the Lord's day and not ours. We are not forsaking gatherings but rather we are redefining the purpose for the gatherings. As we gather together, we are in fellowship with one another. As we leave the church building to go door to door, we are still in fellowship, encouraging one another and together doing what pleases our Father. Bonds made in the fox hole are greater than anywhere else.

Q: Isn't this just one way of spreading the gospel and therefore should not be imposed on any congregation?

We all agree this is just one of the ways. It is not an imposition. It should be done from the heart and not done to impress people. Any congregation should participate after deliberate prayer and asking God if there is a better plan that can deploy its members in masses to accomplish the Great Commission. Whatever you do, please get out of the church building and go to where the people are. The Great Physician seeks out the sick and makes house calls. Let's go seek and save the lost by the gospel of Christ.

Q: Can't we do this on any other day than a Sunday?

Good luck! It is worth trying and has been done and some congregations are doing so even now. Sarcasm aside, see how many would participate on a Saturday when they are busy running errands and/or catching up on the latest entertainment, movies, games and tournaments. You will never have a critical mass gathering of believers on any day other than Sunday. Weekdays are out of the question because of work and other duties.

Q: Shouldn't we respect people's privacy, especially on Sunday?

Yes, we must respect people and be very polite and not be condescending. However, it is disrespectful to say, "Let's just leave them alone. After all, it is their business and their lives." It is like the firefighters saying, "Oh lady, your house is on fire. But we will just let you rest because it is your house. Or maybe we will just come to your house to see if you want to come out from a burning house and maybe we can negotiate with you." The firefighters without hesitation rush to save the lives inside of the burning house and carry them out alive without asking the people if they want to come out of a burning house. The gospel method is very offensive and in your face and we must get used to it. The Word of God first offends and then convicts us of sin. This is the work of the Holy Spirit and not our job.

Q: I am more comfortable with friendship evangelism. How effective can it be talking to total strangers?

It is not either/or. Each has its place and friendship evangelism must be continued by all believers. However, going door to door and two by two is a corporate effort that engages the whole body of Christ and has its place. Yes, people are total strangers, but we are giving them the invitation to meet Jesus, who knows them very well. When Jesus sent His disciples two by two, there is no indication that they knew the people.

Q: People have a strong sense of privacy and protection of their property. Won't it be dangerous to knock on people's doors?

When are we not in danger anyway? If the Lord does not watch a city, then those who watch it labor in vain (see Psalm 127). Our lives are not in our hands. We have nothing to fear according to Jesus (see Matthew 10:28-31).

How about those who went before us and faced greater danger than us? How about the missionaries in very dangerous places who are preaching the gospel? If our only danger is that which we face at the doors of our neighbors, then we need to read apostle Paul's list of dangers in 2 Corinthians 11:23-28.

If the Girl Scouts can knock at the doors to sell their cookies, and if salespeople can knock at doors to sell all kinds of wares, then we have a serious problem as a church if we are afraid of knocking on people's doors to tell them the good news of the gospel. If we knock and someone says to not bother them, then we just go to the next door. Is it dangerous knocking on doors? Yes. It is also dangerous driving out of your garage.

Q: Is the local church the only focus?

The goal is to use all mass gatherings of believers to go and preach the gospel. During conferences and conventions, let's use one of the days of the convention to go out for at least an hour to the immediate community and tell whoever about Jesus.

Q: What about churches with more than one Sunday service?

If the first service is too early in the morning, then we suggest combining it with a later service. We should be considerate of the people we are going to so that we do not wake them up too early.

For later services, also consider combining where it is practical. Some churches have multiple services because of lack of space in the auditorium. If this is the case, consider going out to the community in separate shifts. There is no right or wrong way of going as long it is organized and managed and as long as the gospel is preached by leaving the church building.

Q: What about baby Christians?

New believers, or "baby Christians," are welcome to go out to preach the gospel. It is called on-the-job training. It is called making disciples. Going out with seasoned believers will help new believers understand more clearly what they believe and to be able to articulate in their own words what they know and believe about Jesus and His gospel.

Q: Will people know what to say when confronted?

"For it is not you who will be speaking—it will be the Spirit of your Father speaking through you" (Matthew 10:16-20). Of course, there will be training before you go out. We are not saying that people will be theologians, but they must at least have a relationship with Jesus and understand what He has done in their lives.

Q: One size does not fit all; so what about ministries already doing church outreach?

I am aware that there are many outreach efforts already going on at churches. I am, however, submitting to you that one Sunday a month is not a one-size-fits-all and be all. I believe every ministry and program of the church should be outward-focused.

Q: How can we stay focused on this mission? What about distractions?

We must learn from Jesus. The people who want healing and feeding will look for us to continue to cater to their needs. See how Jesus deals with it in Mark 1:35-39. Jesus always checked in prayer with the Father and thus stayed focused on His mission. We must continuously stay focused on Jesus in prayer and fellowship. As we relate constantly with the Father, we will always discern what is important and when to go, regardless of the demands of the crowd that wants to be catered to.

Q: What about the cultural mix around us?

This question implies that the church building is located in a neighborhood where the majority of the attendees are of a different race than the people who live closest to the church building. The answer is to reach them anyway. Jesus sent us to all, regardless of race, ethnicity or gender. We should never be afraid of reaching people who look different from us. If we hesitate to reach other cultures, we should stop and reevaluate whether we are truly His and what kind of love the Father has put in our hearts.

Matthew 5:44 says to love your enemies. This will take away the fear of approaching people, especially those who don't look like us. If we only go to our neighbors who look like us, then that is not love. Even the pagans do the same.

Q: Isn't speaking to strangers inconvenient and very uncomfortable?

"If indeed we suffer with Him, that we may also be glorified together" (Romans 8:16-17).

When will this scripture be true in our lives? The least of our suffering at this time is approaching strangers.

Q: What if going door to door is contrary to my personality and gifting?

If you are referring to the outgoing personality, the extroverts, I did not read where Jesus said, "For the outgoing personality people, now go to all the world and make disciples." Nor did Christ say, "All you introverts, you can stay home and make disciples in your house or in the church building." In Christ, your personality is secondary. Our primary nature is now spiritual (supernatural) and not natural. We are new creations in Christ, if we have trusted Christ as Lord and Savior. We can no longer depend and act based on our old nature. We now have a God nature and with God all things are possible. All our giftings are for the glory of God. If any gift that we believe God has given us does not glorify Him and point us toward making disciples of Christ, then we must question such gifts. It is not easy for either the extrovert or the introvert to go out and be a witness for Christ. Making disciples is intentional and it is powered by the enablement of the Holy Spirit.

Q: What about weather issues?

Use winter time to teach new believers and do some creative outreach. Use spring, summer and fall to go out as much as you can. Churches in warm climates can go out year-round.

Q: What about overcoming the fear of sharing the gospel?

It is conquered with obedience and stepping out. The fear is of the devil and you must resist him with the Word of God. It doesn't go away just because you have told someone about the gospel before. It comes each time you want to talk about Jesus, especially when it's with someone of a different culture. "For God has not given us a spirit of fear and timidity, but of power, love, and self-discipline" (2 Timothy 1:7).

Q: Can we employ social media in this outreach?

Yes, at two levels. One is with the church members. We should have people's emails or Twitter handles, Facebook connections, or whatever, so that we can share instant messages, changes in plans, and reminders. Depending on how the conversation turns out, we should gently ask and obtain the same information from those we reach at their homes. We already know their addresses, so if they volunteer their cell phone numbers, emails and so on, we can follow up quickly within no more than a week. If they don't wish to give out their email (and people are justified in fearing spam), then we can always use their first names to send a follow-up thank-you note to their address by snail mail.

Q: What about those who only want to stay and pray?

Remind them that they are the answer to their own prayers to send laborers into the field. However, for those who cannot go because of physical limitations, let them stay and pray. The Lord has told me, "You are not to twist anyone's arm. This is My work and I will work on the people and leaders to motivate them. Pray and speak the vision and leave the rest to Me."

Q: Won't people think we're Jehovah's Witnesses?

Tell them that you are not, that you are from their neighborhood church, and that you are not selling any pamphlet or product to them.

Q: What kind of questions should we ask the people?

We should always ask open-ended questions and not questions with yes or no responses. We can ask such questions as, "Where are you on your spiritual/faith journey? What is the most important thing in this world that matters to you? Why?" We must listen carefully and allow them to speak more than we talk. Subsequent questions will come from what they say. It is a conversation and not a debate.

Q: What if they ask hard questions?

Kindly thank them for their insightful questions. If you don't know the answer, then tell them you will find answers to the questions and get back to them. But do not make up answers that will later contradict the Bible. See these as a positive thing and a learning and growing opportunity. The people will be humbled when they see your humility that you don't have all the answers.

Q: What if I disagree with my paired partner on answers given while speaking to the people?

There may from time to time arise tensions between the evangelizing pairs. There may be disagreements. Even if you disagree with your partner on something that comes up in a conversation with the person being visited, do *not* show any tension or anything other than unity. You should, however, talk about your disagreements subsequently in brotherly love.

Q: What about those who come to church for the first time on the evangelism outreach Sunday?

This is a good question because it gives the opportunity to tell them the gospel. If they are already Christ followers, then they can join you to go out if they choose to. Otherwise they can stay and pray with those praying.

Q: If this is during a conference, who do you pair together?

Try to pair men with men and women with women. If couples are attending, they should be paired together.

Q: What kind of record of the visit do we keep?

Upon leaving and not in front of the people, you should record and note addresses, reactions, names if given, and issues to pray for.

Q: Do we invite them to church?

Yes, if they show interest. Our primary mission is to introduce them to Christ and invite them to a relationship with God, their Maker.

Q: What kind of places should people attending large conferences and retreats go to preach?

They can go to the streets downtown or to any public place where they can encounter lots of people. They can equally go to homes where it is practical. Working with local churches in the area is critical for follow-up and success.

Q: How do you refer converts to local churches when on a conference or retreat outreach?

Ahead of such outreaches, plans must be made to involve the local churches in the area. Any follow-up and information gathered should be passed on to the local churches.

Q: When they come to church, how do we identify them?

Hopefully those who spoke to them will keep in touch with the people, especially if they showed interest in coming to church. You should look out for them, welcome them, and make them feel comfortable. Introduce the newcomer to other believers in the church.

Q: What about subsequent visits after the first? Who should join in next-month outreach to the community?

We should continue to go and make disciples. It is not just a one-day event. It is a lifetime commitment. It takes multiple exposures to the gospel for people to be awakened. That has been my experience and it probably will be the same for you. Believers will be so excited after the first outing that they will ask why they have not done this till now. More people will join in subsequent visits and those who have gone before should invite other believers who have yet to do so.

Q: What should we expect?

Expect miracles of new life in Christ and others things, such as healing and restoration of families and restoration of broken lives.

Q: How do we measure outreach success?

We are not solely after numbers, but the early church showed growth by numbers. Many were added to the church. We must have a real measure of growth. Yes, some will say it is a spiritual matter and growth cannot be quantified, but that is not how the New Testament viewed it.

I believe that after some time, we should notice some increase in the number of new believers being baptized. We must be patient and obedient to planting and watering the seeds and let God bring the growth and increase.

Q: What is the Gospel Message?

1 Corinthians 15:1-8 summarized the gospel message. All humans have sinned and deserve hell punishment. Jesus who is Himself God, came to earth as a human and died for our sins that we can be forgiven. He was buried and rose from the dead and ascended into heaven. He is coming back again to take those who believe and receive Him as Lord and Savior. Those who do not believe and receive Jesus, condemn themselves to eternal hell and separation from God.

A Prayer for the Church

Lord, I thank You for choosing and electing us before the world began. It is an overwhelming thought and realization. Thank You for calling each of us by Your name and for Your glory.

Father, we thank You for Your only begotten Son, Jesus Christ, who died on the cross for us and adopted us into Your family, the church. We thank You for the disciples who came before us and who were obedient to Your commands to go and preach the gospel to all the world and to every creature. We came to You through their obedience. We have received the good news of You and of Your saving faith that comes by hearing Your Word.

We confess our sins of disobedience, the loss of our first love, and the loss of the things we did when we first came to know and trust You. We repent of our sins and of our incestuous lifestyle. Forgive us, Lord; we pray this day. Renew us with Your right Spirit.

Now we pray that You help and empower us all to walk in obedience to Your Great Commission. Help us to see with Your eyes and hear Your heart for the perishing. Grant us the same compassion You experienced when You saw the people like sheep without a shepherd. Help us to look out and see that the harvest is ready and not to say that there are still four months left. Lord, please remove the spiritual blindness of our neighbors and all people we encounter with the truth of Your Gospel that they will believe and be reconciled to You.

Lord, we pray that You send forth from all churches workers into Your harvest field. Lord, help us to be the answer to this prayer that Jesus asked us to pray for the workers.

Thank You for the leaders of the church. We pray that You give them and all of us the boldness to lead the church to obedience.

Lord, help us to embrace with joy the sufferings of this life for the sake of You and Your gospel.

We commit to You this proposed idea of using at least one Sunday a month to go out and preach the gospel to our neighbors. Empower us to do this and to preach the gospel. Empower us to employ every available means to "go and make disciples" for You.

We confess all our fears of what people will say and think of us. Help us to believe and attempt the impossible, for with You, nothing is impossible. Help us to love one another and take care of one another.

Lord, strengthen our faith and help us to comprehend Your love for us. We pray now as Paul prayed for the Ephesians:

> For this reason, I kneel before the Father, from whom every family in heaven and on earth derives its name. I pray that out of his glorious riches he may strengthen you with power through his Spirit in your inner being, so that Christ may dwell in your hearts through faith. And I pray that you, being rooted and established in love, may have power, together with all the Lord's holy people, to grasp how wide and long and high and deep is the love of Christ, and to know this love that surpasses knowledge—that you may be filled to the measure of all the fullness of God.
>
> Now to him who is able to do immeasurably more than all we ask or imagine, according to his power that is at work within us, to him be glory in the church and in Christ Jesus throughout all generations, for ever and ever! Amen. (Ephesians 3:14-20)

Acknowledgments

Thank you, Pastor Phil Powers, for preaching the "Radical" series. Thank you for your encouragement and for your prayers. You have done your part. God, through all of us, is working out His purposes through the church. Likewise, thanks to David Platt, whose book *Radical* inspired Pastor Phil.

Special thanks go to my dear lovely wife, UD, who was the first person to read my very first rough draft. Your comments on tone helped guide the rest of my writing and revisions. God has given us wives for sensitivity, and I appreciate this gift in UD. Honey, you and our children, Jonathan and Grace, have been so kind, loving and caring during my stroke recovery and in the writing of this book. Thank you for your sacrifices and for sharing in my passion to reach many for Christ. I thank God for the gift of the three of you. This past year has been the most difficult but, at the same time, the most impacting and rewarding.

Along the same line, my sincere thanks to our family friend Lovette Ego and my sister-in-law Ogechi Okehielem, who both read my very rough drafts. Your honest comments and issues raised helped me with the wisdom to generate and answer critical questions/objections that would arise in anyone's mind regarding going out at least one Sunday a month.

Another thank-you goes to my friend and brother in Christ Isaac Megbelugbe. Even in your lowest moments, when most would have settled into self-pity and grief for your dear wife and our sister in Christ, Josephine, you found strength to give your time to review my manuscript. You asked me serious questions that led to a better product of organized thoughts and writing. Your professional and academic approach to reviewing my writing has paid many dividends.

My sincere thanks also to my brother in Christ Steve D'Alessio for reading the manuscript and for your honest feedback on content and tone. I appreciate your support and friendship and for going door to door with me.

Likewise, I thank my dear brother in Christ Josh Biber, who has faithfully and consistently gone door to door with me in testing and proving that this way of evangelism works and that it is effective. Josh, you are precious.

I thank my brother in Christ, evangelist Paul Adams of the Open Air Campaigners USA. I learned so much from your boldness in proclaiming Christ on the streets of downtown Silver Spring. Also, thank you for believing in door to door and for the times we did it together. May the Lord continue to advance your ministry in saving souls for Christ.

I have so many more people to thank both in the writing process and through my stroke recovery: friends, family members, caregivers, church home-group members and pastors, my co-workers and my workplace Bible study group (the Ambassadors of Christ). Some of you read some of my writings, listened to me, and encouraged me as I shared the concept with you. You know yourselves, and I say, may the Lord bless you. Thank you all for your prayers and for your care. I thank God for all of you.

Last, I thank my editor, Julia Duin. It is a miracle how God made me aware of you through one of your books. God used you to nudge me into putting my best efforts into this book. Your wealth of experience as a follower of Christ and as a journalist in the print media business has brought the best into your editing and counsel on producing this book. Thank you, Julia!

Bibliography

Baptist Board Forum, "Is door-to-door evangelism soliciting?" December 4, 2013. Retrieved from https://www.baptistboard.com/threads/is-door-to-door-evangelism-soliciting.84916/

Bradley, Jayson, "5 Ways to start a Conversation about the Gospel." Jesus Film Project, Feb. 14, 2017. Retrieved from https://www.jesusfilm.org/blog-and-stories/conversation-about-gospel.html.

Casting Crowns, "Oh My Soul," March 10, 2017. Retrieved from https://www.you tube.com/watch?v=DjNZf878ISQ

Chambers, Oswald, "The Key to the Missionary's Work." *My Utmost for His Highest*, Oct. 14, 2017. Retrieved from https://utmost.org/the-key-to-the-missionarys-work/.

Chambers, Oswald, "The Highest Good—The Pilgrim's Song Book." *Wisdom from Oswald Chambers*, https://utmost.org/quotes/2331/

Clifton, Mark, *Reclaiming Glory: Revitalizing Dying Churches*. B&H Publishing Group, Nashville, Tenn.: 2016, 16-17.

Cornetet, Robin, "Mythbuster, Louisville Pastor Triples Attendance in 6 Months by Knocking on Doors." *Kentucky Today*, Aug. 27, 2017. Retrieved from http://kentuckytoday.com/stories/mythbuster-louisville-pastor-triples-attendance-in-6-months-by-knocking-on-doors,8782.

Dodson, Jonathan, "Evangelism on the Rocks." *DesiringGod.org*, February 12, 2015. Retrieved from https://www.desiringgod.org/articles/evangelism-on-the-rocks.

Doyle, Tom, *Standing in the Fire: Courageous Christians Living in Frightening Times*. W Publishing Group, Nashville, Tenn., 2017, 1-24.

Duin, Julia, *Quitting Church: Why the Faithful Are Fleeing and What to Do About It*. Baker Books, Grand Rapids, Mich., 2008.

Guzik, David, "Study Guide for Luke 9." *The Blue Letter Bible*, Feb. 21, 2017. Retrieved from https://www.blueletterbible.org/Comm/guzik_david/StudyGuide2017-Luk/Luk-9.cfm.

Evangelical Christian Credit Union, Investing in Ministry, "2013 Church Budget Allocations, Learning Priorities, and Quarterly Financial Trends." Retrieved from http://web.archive.org/web/20141019033209/https:/www.eccu.org/resources/advisorypanel/2013/surveyreports20.

Jeske, Mark; *Time of Grace*, Fox 5 Plus-WDCA Channel 20 Television, July 9, 2017.

Lynn, Sheryl, "Here is Why Christians Don't Share Their Faith." *The Christian Post*, July 14, 2017. Retrieved from https://www.christianpost.com/news/heres-why-christians-dont-share-their-faith-chuck-lawless-192012/.

Mowry, Bill, *The Ways of the Alongsider: Growing Disciples Life2Life*. NavPress, Colorado Springs, Colo., 2012, 17.

Neighbour, Randall, "How to Successfully Launch a Holistic Small Group (cell group) Ministry." *TOUCH,* http://www.touchusa.org/content/launchgroups.asp

Nwachukwu, Udo, "A Good Stroke—Update and Thank You." August 6, 2016. *House2HouseMD,* http://house2housemd.blogspot.com/

Premier Christian Radio, "The Profile: Nabeel Qureshi's Conversion from Islam to Christianity." Retrieved from https://www.premierchristianradio.com/Shows/Saturday/The-Profile/The-Profile-Podcast/The-Profile-Nabeel-Qureshi-s-conversion-from-Islam-to-Christianity

Sheehan, Ryan, "3500 People Leave the Church Every Day." *The Christian Post*, May 27, 2017. Retrieved from www.christianpost.com news/3500-people-leave-the-church-every-day-139631.

The Restoration of the Gospel of Jesus Christ, Intellectual Reserve Inc., The Church of Jesus Christ of Latter-Day Saints, 2008, 15.

Tice, Rico, *Honest Evangelism: How to talk about Jesus when it's tough.* The Good Book Company Croydon, U.K., 2015, 48.

Tozer, A. W., "Revival: It Requires Obedience." *The Size of the Soul: Principles of Revival and Spiritual Growth*, compiled by Harry Verploegh. Wing Spread, Camp Hill, Pa., 2010, 18-19.

Qureshi, Nabeel, *Seeking Allah, Finding Jesus: A Devout Muslim Encounters Christianity*. Zondervan Publishing, Grand Rapids, Mich., 2014.

Rainer, Thom, "Dispelling the 80 Percent Myth of Declining Churches." *Thom S. Rainer*, June 28, 2017. https://thomrainer.com/2017/06/dispelling-80-percent-myth-declining-churches/.

Wong, Alicia, "Is Door-to-door Evangelism Worth It?" *Biblical Woman*, Feb. 16, 2016. http://biblicalwoman.com/door-to-door-evangelism/.

Wood, David, "The Life and Death of Nabeel Qureshi." *Christian World News Interview*, September 23, 2017, online video, YouTube, https://www.youtube.com/watch?v=Ca6m3dMACjc.

Yoffie, Eric H., "Why Americans Dismiss Sin." *The Huffington Post*, Dec. 20, 2011. Retrieved from https://www.huffingtonpost.com/rabbi-eric-h-yoffie/why-americans-dismiss-sin_ b_1018284.html.

Zacharias, Ravi, *"Nabeel Qureshi, 1983-2017."* RZIM News Magazine, published by Ravi Zacharias International Ministries, Autumn 2017, p. 2. Also, "Ravi Zacharias Eulogy at Nabeel Qureshi's Funeral" at https://www.youtube.com/watch?v=Iq2kdVYt3A8.

Zacharias, Ravi, "Doctrine of Hell and the Eternality of Hell." RZIM.org Radio program *Let My People Think*: "The Pursuit of Meaning: Regaining the Wonder, Part 2." Posted by Ravi Zacharias International Ministries, Dec. 9, 2017.

Zaimov, Stoyan, "Born-Again Christians Continue Declining, Only Minority Believe They Must Share the Gospel: Survey." *The Christian Post*, Dec. 1, 2017. Retrieved from http://www.christianpost.com/news/born-again-christians-continue-declining-only-minority-believe-they-must-share-the-gospel-survey-208559/.

Zauzmer, Julie, "Fishing for Another 'Like': At Easter, many Christians return to door-to-door methods." *The Washington Post*, March 30, 2018. Retrieved from https://www.washingtonpost.com/news/acts-of-faith/wp/2018/03/30/ditching-facebook-at-easter-many-christians-return-to-door-to-door-methods/?utm_campaign=988f979d67-EMAIL_CAMPAIGN_2018_03_30&utm_medium=email&utm_source=Pew%20Research%20Center&utm_term=.31fd9bdb897a.

About the Author

Udo F. Nwachukwu is a marketplace minister who has led a Bible study group called the Ambassadors of Christ at his workplace for more than 23 years. He believes there is no secular versus sacred calling. Udo was born in Abia state, Nigeria, was apprehended by Christ at the age of 17, put his faith and trust in his Lord and Savior, and has never looked back.

Udo moved to the United States in 1980 to attend Marquette University in Wisconsin, then Howard University in Washington, DC, where he graduated with a BA in accounting. He has been a CPA since 1985 and now works as a U.S. government employee.

Udo later attended Regent University in Virginia Beach, Virginia, where he earned his master's degree in practical theology. He has served the body of Christ in many capacities as elder and board member, house church leader, and just plain witness for Christ in his community and spheres of influence.

Udo is married to his lovely wife, UD, and they enjoy the company of their two children, Jonathan and Grace. They live in Silver Spring, Maryland.

Udo invites you to visit his blog (www.house2housemd.blog spot.com) and website (www.udoministries.com). He can be emailed at ambassador2dworld@gmail.com.